# Friends in Deed

Dear Gail

A little light reading
for my "friend in deed"

Love,
Linda

# Friends in Deed

## Stories About Acts of Kindness

**DIMENSIONS**

FOR LIVING

NASHVILLE

FRIENDS IN DEED

First Dimensions for Living edition 1997

97 98 99 00 01 02 03 04 05 06 — 10 9 8 7 6 5 4 3 2 1

MANUFACTURED IN THE UNITED STATES OF AMERICA

*Whenever we have an opportunity,
let us work for the good of all . . . .*

Galatians 6:10 (NRSV)

# CONTENTS

# CONTENTS

# CONTENTS

# CONTENTS

HELPING HANDS

# PREFACE

These inspiring stories, compiled by the editors of *Guideposts*, are about real people who found practical ways to bring happiness into the lives of others. They represent a wide variety of backgrounds, but they have this in common: They noticed a need, and when they put their ordinary skills, hobbies, or interests to work, they discovered that they could make an *extra*ordinary difference in their world.

You will read about

- the woman who baked made-to-order cakes for children at a local hospital;
- the man who read news stories to blind people over the telephone;
- the loan officer who found work for people who had lost their jobs;
- the girl who wrote encouraging letters to people she had never met;

13

- the elevator mechanic who used old parts to build a neighborhood gym for kids; and
- the sewing enthusiast who created doll clothes for children—plus many more stories of people reaching out to others in their own unique ways.

There is nothing superhuman or superspiritual about the people in this book; they simply saw a need, were moved by it, and decided to do something about it. Through their human hands they put God's love into action.

Those hands could be *your* hands. Just read on. In these stories you will discover a world of simple—yet effective—ways that *you*, too, can be a friend in deed.

# A FRIENDLY PAW-SHAKE

In England, most of the nursing homes where Elaine Smith worked as a registered nurse had a pet or mascot. That was when she first noticed the effect a friendly animal could have on elderly people who had become withdrawn and unresponsive.

Later, after Elaine had moved to Hillside, New Jersey—and acquired a sweet-tempered and well-trained German shepherd—she read a newspaper story about a woman who had taken her dog to visit nursing home patients. It was just the nudge Elaine needed. And so she began an unusual ministry with her dog, Phila, whose name in Greek means "love."

From their very first visit to a local nursing home, it was apparent that a friendly paw-shake and a wagging tail were often just what the doctor ordered for the patients who no longer seemed to care about being alive. As Phila went through her paces—obeying word and hand signals, jumping a hurdle, retrieving a glove—Elaine saw new interest begin to shine in patients' eyes.

The more nursing homes and hospitals Elaine and Phila visited, the more they seemed to get special results. "One elderly woman hadn't spoken a word for years," Elaine remembers. "Then one day she sat up, put out her hands, and said, 'Phila, here, Phila.'" Still another, a ninety-year-old, had become reclusive and wouldn't leave her room. But when she heard that a dog was coming to visit, she was up and ready, the first person in the welcoming line. Therapists at the various facilities kept telling Elaine that, after a session with her dog, the patients were often more responsive to *people*.

Eventually, Elaine began to toy with an idea. She knew there were already many dog clubs, schools, and individuals who voluntarily took their affectionate, well-trained pets to visit not only the elderly, but also children and grown-ups confined to hospitals for long stays. So with the help of some good friends, Elaine founded Therapy Dogs International (TDI). The purpose was to recognize, unite, and increase the number of canine "therapists," and also to alert institutions worldwide to the value and availability of these dogs.

Word of the new organization spread rapidly, and Elaine became optimistic that one day therapy dogs would be commonplace. She could see the benefits they bring to people who are separated from family, friends, and their own pets.

—Odean Cusack

# THE ANIMAL NURSE

Please, Mommy, make it well."

Joe Trindal blinked back tears as he held up an injured hummingbird.

His mother, Mary, had no idea how to care for a bird of any kind, but she and her young son had the same gentle, compassionate feelings about wildlife. "I'll try," she said.

And try she did. That one tiny bird was the first of hundreds of God's helpless creatures who, over the years, found refuge at Mary's house in Alexandria, Virginia. For decades, neighbors and strangers alike came to her door with hurt or orphaned birds and small woodland animals.

From the beginning, Mary had an unexpected talent for "nursing" wild creatures. Her secret? Gentle hands, tender care, and prayer. "I always pray for guidance in handling them," she said. "My goal is to return them to the wild and free life God intended them to have."

Over the years, Mary tracked down veterinarians willing to help and found other people in her community to take these "patients" into their homes to recuperate. Eventually she managed to organize a network of volunteers, each specializing in the care of a particular animal.

Mary herself became the "raccoon person." Her most memorable raccoon boarder was sent to her to convalesce after being hit by a car. But the animal hated captivity and refused to eat, earning the nickname Grouchy. As days passed, he grew weaker.

Afraid Grouchy would die, Mary said a prayer and took him to a woodland feeding station that volunteers had set up for animals readjusting to life in the wild. But Grouchy wasn't safe there, either. Heavy rains flooded the station. A volunteer reported seeing the raccoon lying on the wet ground, feverish, panting, and presumably near death. When Mary was able to visit the station, expecting to bury Grouchy, she found him up on his paws—shaky, but obviously on his way to health and freedom.

Mary also worked to educate people about the American timber wolf, which almost became extinct. "It's one of the most maligned and persecuted of all creatures," she said.

The leap from hummingbird to wolves was not an improbable one for Mary. In her words, "They're both precious links in God's chain of life."

# ANTIQUE THE CLOWN

A fragile old woman. A smiling clown. The clown put white-gloved hands on the old woman's shoulders, and they became bound in a warm hug, united in good cheer. They were in a nursing home, but on that day the place was as happy as any circus big top.

Edna Belle Poole—yes, a woman—was the clown, and to see her move irrepressibly through the nursing home—dancing, miming, smiling, and embracing—you would think she had never known a dark day in her life. But not too many years before, Edna had lived alone in a Phoenix, Arizona, apartment—unmarried, desolate, and on the verge of a nervous breakdown. Until then Edna had devoted her best energies to caring for her beloved mother, Anna. When Anna died at age ninety-four, Edna suddenly felt unneeded and empty.

Through the prayers and caring support of friends, Edna was encouraged to find a pursuit that would occupy all the time she had once spent caring for her mother. What could she do? What could she give that people really needed? Well, she was naturally gregarious and liked to cheer people up. Why not be a clown?

Edna acquired a bright and baggy clown suit, had a theater-trained friend help her make up a whimsical face, and thus went out into the world as Antique the Clown. (Why "Antique"? Years earlier Edna had been known as Antique to her young nieces and nephews. *Aunt*-ique!)

Edna/Antique began visiting pediatric wards, homes for those with mental disabilities, civic charity functions, nursing homes, and a women's prison. To each place she brought balloons and pockets full of trinkets and candy.

Remarkably, Edna fit this clowning into an already busy schedule. She held down a full-time position at Maricopa Community Colleges in Phoenix, gave time to her church, St. Stephen's Episcopal, and also volunteered at a Phoenix historical society.

Since she refused to accept any payment for her clowning, it was not surprising that Edna was once honored as "Volunteer of the Year" by the state of Arizona. When asked how she managed to do it all, Edna said, "God and the memory of my mother led me to do this. That's what got me started. And once you're under way, you would be amazed at how far you can go on the smiles of others."

—Lois Jamieson

# ANYTHING FOR MISS SHELLY

If you had seen a picture that was taken of a special group of students at Miss Shelly's School of Dance in Tulsa, Oklahoma, they wouldn't have seemed much different from other dance school pupils—giggly and starry-eyed. On closer inspection, you would have noticed one girl with a walker, another wearing a leg brace, a third in a wheelchair. The youngsters were physically and mentally challenged—with spina bifida, muscular dystrophy, mental retardation, and other disabilities. Yet Miss Shelly taught them to dance.

Shelly Ledbetter began teaching the class when Jennifer Hardy, a young girl with physical disabilities, pulled herself up to the ballet bar and began swaying to the music. Convinced that dance could help the child's range of motion and flexibility, Shelly offered to give the girl lessons. She consulted a physical therapist and then opened a class—free of charge for all children with disabilities.

The students, as many as twenty-two at a time, waltzed to Strauss melodies, did the rumba to "La Bamba," swayed their hands, and shuffled their feet. They even gave a recital every

21

year. They gained confidence, poise, and a willingness to take risks.

Ten-year-old Mindy Barry had cerebral palsy and could walk only by using leg braces. Her mother said, "We never dreamed we'd see Mindy on stage—not until Miss Shelly's class. It's given her a boost in self-esteem. Mindy will try things in ballet that would terrify her in therapy. She'd do *anything* for Miss Shelly."

Shelly explained that the challenge was to choreograph dance routines tailor-made for the children's abilities. "Instead of looking at what they can't do," she said, "I try to see what they *can* do."

Using her God-given talent to teach was something Shelly Ledbetter could do—and she did it well.

—Melanie Arnold Hemry

# BLOOMING WITH COLOR

One evening John Feight was showing some patients how painting is done—part of his weekly volunteer work in the mental health section of Northside Hospital in Atlanta, Georgia. Glancing up at the plain, unadorned walls of the dining room, he got an idea.

"Hey," he said to the people gathered around his easel, "let's see if we can get permission to paint murals on the blank walls!"

The patients were enthusiastic—and so was the hospital administration. John supplied the art materials and the directions: "We'll paint what we think might be out there on the other side of the wall," he told his pajama-clad assistants.

Soon the drab walls of the room bloomed with color. And when the medical staff noticed the brightening effect on patients' morale, John's landscapes, seascapes, jungle animals, and still lifes began filling up the space between floors and ceilings in area after area throughout the hospital. Soon Northside had more than five hundred murals. John began to lead mural-painting groups in dozens of other hospitals.

Whenever he painted, John invited patients to help. The prospect of working with him was often such good medicine that people made an effort to get out of their beds to brush a tail on a smiling giraffe or daub in a sky or sunset. "It's easier when they aren't artists to start with—they have wonderful, fresh ideas," he said.

Though committed to his art, John made his career in business as manager of marketing communications for an international electronics firm. Since his job called for considerable travel, he found ways to continue his cooperative murals at hospitals across America and in Europe.

Where did his desire to help others come from? It runs in the family. While growing up in Killbuck, Ohio, he watched his grandfather, a country doctor, give medicine, advice, and help to people, even though many could not afford to pay. John chose to donate his time and talent—in some cases, he even contributed the painting supplies.

"Service to others is a way of showing love, which comes from God," John said. "Doing these hospital murals gives me inner peace and a sense of purpose for my life."

—Janet Shaffer

# MOTHER GOOSE

The sick and terminally ill children in the pediatrics wing of Sutter Memorial Hospital in Sacramento, California, had a friend: Mother Goose. She was really Frances Reimer Burt, a middle-aged former schoolteacher and well-known local artist who devoted much of her talent and time to brightening the lives of the little patients. Carrying a huge bag filled with surprises and wearing a big, black hat, Mrs. Burt made her rounds. In late October and at Christmastime she would appear in seasonal costumes, but most of the year she was simply Mother Goose.

In her "magic apron" she carried such wonders as a golden egg, a mouse that ran up a clock, a small Billy Goat Gruff, or a troll with long, fuzzy hair and popping eyes. Out of the enormous bag came homemade hand puppets and a mechanical goose that waddled in crazy circles. Mother Goose took out her colored chalk and set up her easel at each child's bed, one after the other.

"So what shall I draw you today?" she asked. Linda wanted "a beach with sea gulls and a boat on the ocean." Jeff requested "a green monster with fangs." For two hours the children got their pictures—but for two hours only, because Mrs. Burt's hands were crippled by arthritis and tired easily.

Mother Goose told the children that she came to them by flying "through the air on a very large gander," but actually she came by bus. Her doctor was always warning her to stay off her feet, for her ankles swelled painfully when she stood too long, waiting for a bus to arrive. But Mrs. Burt persisted in her hospital work.

"Sometimes I wonder why," she said. "Occasionally I think I should be home, watching television or baking cookies for my grandchildren. And then I remember a little boy in a wheelchair and a little girl just out of her third skin graft operation, and I think of how my own children grew up strong and healthy. God gave me talent to draw. Surely I have an obligation to show my gratitude by giving a few kids some moments of happiness. Anyhow—I enjoy it. It's a great thing to pull a bit of magic from my apron and trade it for a child's smile."

—Charlotte Hutchison

# THE "PLAY LADY"

A gray December morning—a chilly rain falling—it was just a few days before Christmas.

For the twenty-three children in the Pediatrics Unit at Memorial Medical Center in Savannah, Georgia, the brief flurry of weekend visitors was over. Monday in the hospital had just begun. Like most hospital patients, the children were facing another week of boredom or pain. But there was one bright spot. They knew the "Play Lady" was coming.

Meanwhile, in a public housing development on the other side of the city, Carolyn White was bundling up for the cold walk to the bus stop. She carried a grocery bag packed with toys and games she had collected as donations from local businesses. The round-trip bus fare was a sizable sum for a person with limited income, but no matter. The Play Lady was on her way to spend a rainy Monday with her children.

Her "children" were the three thousand youngsters admitted each year to Memorial Medical Center. For those children— some hospitalized for critical illness, some neglected, some abused—the arrival of this warmhearted volunteer was the high point of the day.

Social or economic backgrounds made no difference to the smiling woman; she cuddled and loved the children as if they were her own. She spent thirty to forty hours each week in the third-floor playroom at Memorial, organizing play and craft activities, and decorating walls and corridors with brightly colored scenes and mobiles that the children had created.

In her spare time Carolyn went from shop to shop in the downtown area, asking merchants to donate toys or materials for handcrafts. Some refused, but many others listened, and usually Carolyn came home with a shopping bag full of crayons or green felt for making Christmas cards, or red paper for valentines. When children couldn't leave their hospital beds— and many could not—the Play Lady took games or activities to their bedsides. At the end of every day she cleaned and disinfected the toys that had been used. When occupancy in the Pediatrics Unit was high, she recruited additional volunteers for the playroom.

Once Carolyn was named "Volunteer of the Year" and presented with an award by Mayor John P. Rousakis in a special ceremony. "I didn't do it by myself," she said. "When I woke up this morning I was singing a song in my heart, 'To God Be the Glory.' I rejoice in that song today."

Nurses, physicians—everyone at Memorial loved the Play Lady. Said staff member Jeryl Davis, "A lot of people hesitate to become volunteers because they think you need some kind of grand social standing or independent income. Carolyn White proves that notion is totally wrong. All you need is the desire and determination to help others—and a warm and loving heart."

# A SAFE PLACE TO PLAY

During the day Tony Dalton worked as an elevator mechanic in a midtown Manhattan skyscraper. But at night he could be seen lifting elevator gears—old, discarded ones from work—that he had fashioned into weights for a gym in New York City's south Bronx.

That's where Tony was born. He went to school and church there and played in its streets. In the 1960s, as the people of his working-class neighborhood began leaving, Tony remained. He watched, appalled, as apartment buildings were emptied, boarded up, even burned down by arsonists. He hated to see his neighborhood looking like a bombed-out war zone.

One day when he saw a junkie hurling a brick from the roof of an abandoned building, barely missing a child playing in an alley below, Tony decided something had to be done to create a safe place for kids. He went to his parish church, St. Rita's, and talked to his pastor. Because of decreasing attendance and increasing fuel costs, the nave of the church had been walled off, and half of it was being used for storage. Tony wanted to turn that area into a gym.

The pastor agreed, and Tony went to work. With the help of a fireman friend, Jim Myerjack, and about twenty teenagers, Tony emptied the storage area of its debris, then washed and painted the roof, walls, and floor.

Tony then built backboards for seventeen basketball rims and installed them. He made frames for Ping-Pong tables and benches for weight lifters. For the smaller children, he mounted a basketball rim on a backboard six feet from the ground. In one section he hung an old telephone pole, suspended punching bags from it, and added ladder bars for gymnastics. It took him more than a year; he had to build it in the evenings, on his days off, and on vacations.

Tony opened the gym at St. Rita's to a crowd of impatient youngsters, and it was a huge success, being used by more than two hundred children from the ages of five to nineteen.

Every evening after work Tony went there to supervise. He would referee a basketball game or coach a beginning gymnast or spar a little with a pint-sized boxer. The rules were few—no smoking, no swearing, and no fighting outside the ring—and they were strictly observed.

Every evening before he opened the doors, Tony asked God to "see that the kids have fun without getting hurt, and guide them home safely." And before long, the kids were praying with him.

—Sidney Fields

# "My Doll"

Five-year-old Susie was very weak—so weak that her doctor at the Children's Home didn't think she would live until Christmas. So Susie was given a doll early. Quietly she lay in her crib, cuddling the doll tightly against her cheek.

"She seemed to get better as soon as she got the doll," her doctor later told the woman known as "the Doll Lady." "Susie kept looking at the doll and murmuring, '*My* doll, *my* doll.' I think it must have been the first thing of her own she'd ever had. Evidently, having the doll gave her the will to live."

For fifteen years the Doll Lady had been sending dolls to hospitals and schools for children who were crippled, sick, or disabled. Each doll was beautifully dressed with hand-sewn clothes, and each of the garments was different.

Every January the Doll Lady began to dress the dolls for the following Christmas—a dozen a month for nine months of the year. It took about twelve hours to complete one doll, since many had crocheted or knitted hats, collars, or edgings. And then there were the bonus dolls.

"After I finish my quota of a dozen each month, I dress a larger doll for a wheelchair child. That's an extra bonus of pleasure for myself every month."

"Why don't you sell me one?" a friend once asked, thinking that the money from the sale would help the children.

"The dolls are just for the sick children. I could give money, too, but working and sewing on the clothes means I'm giving a part of myself," the Doll Lady explained.

Some of the material for the clothing was donated by friends, and, as his contribution to the work, the Doll Lady's husband paid for all the dolls.

Reared in the Quaker tradition, the Doll Lady was taught as a young child the fundamental Quaker characteristic of service. She served others through Quaker relief societies, the Red Cross, her church organizations, and—in her late seventies— through her dolls for the children.

No one knew the name of the Doll Lady except hospital and school officials. "That would spoil the gift," she explained. "A complete gift is one that is given to someone unknown, and the giver must remain anonymous. Being called 'The Doll Lady' is enough of a name for me."

# CARE FOR THE CHILDREN

Holidays at Folsom—California's maximum security prison—could be dismal, especially for the children of inmates. The youngsters arrived wide-eyed and scared as they passed through clanging metal gates under the watchful eyes of armed guards. Once inside, they visited with fathers who were often strangers to them.

One bright figure in that otherwise bleak scene was Shirley Neff, a smiling, five-foot woman who presided over the "Welcome House" playground, a Volunteers of America program within the prison. Shirley, a former travel agent who had raised four children of her own, took the job after terrorism scares caused many layoffs in the tourist industry.

One of the first things Shirley did was design a coloring book that explained why Dad was in prison. "The children must grapple with the idea that their fathers are bad men," she said. "I tell them, 'No, your father did a bad thing.'"

After the children had visited their fathers, they went to the playground. That gave their parents some time alone. Shirley and her small staff of volunteers from the local Jesuit High

School cared for fifteen to twenty-six children, five days a week. "We work very hard on self-esteem," she said. "We have few rules, but they're consistently enforced: no fighting, no bad language, put the toys away when you're finished."

Infractions were remedied by a "time out" meeting with Neff in her office. Before the children could leave, however, they had to give Shirley a hug. "These kids need a lot of love and discipline to keep from ending up here themselves," she said.

Welcome House also provided other services, including transportation, parenting classes for the inmates, and a support program for their girlfriends and wives. And Shirley developed a prerelease class for inmates called "Tough Love and Reality Training."

"It offers clues for what to do on the outside," she said. "I tell them to believe in themselves and not to be limited by the past. Some of the men in Folsom will never get out, and they probably never should. But others have lived desperate lives and are willing to change if someone can show them another way."

Shirley Neff helped show them that way.

# JUST PLAIN LISTENING

Once a week Winnie went to work. It was a demanding, nine-to-six job in a bustling New York office that never closed—Monday through Sunday, twenty-four hours a day. The phones were always ringing and Winnie answered them; but she didn't coax, cajole, wheel, or deal. She didn't put people on hold or tell them to call back later. Her job was to listen.

Winnie was not paid for her work. She was a volunteer at Help Line, an over-the-phone crisis-intervention center in New York City. She was one of the thousands of Americans who volunteer to help with hot lines—listening to the problems of people who are desperate, lonely, confused, and depressed. And because of the promise of anonymity, they are able to reach people who are afraid to talk to anyone else.

Winnie became a Help Line volunteer in the late sixties, at her husband's suggestion. "He flattered me by telling me he thought I'd be good at it," she said. A former nurse, she had long been accustomed to using her listening skills. But at Help Line she was soon using them in a new way.

Through the intensive training that Help Line provided, Winnie learned the concept of "active listening." This is a therapeutic method of listening carefully, asking key questions, getting a caller to focus on the root of his or her problem, and then helping the individual find the understanding that will lead to its solution.

"Ninety percent of what our callers need is just plain listening," Winnie said. And the other ten percent? "It's the encouragement to find something they can do to help themselves. Even the smallest baby step they can take on their own is better than any advice we can give."

At Help Line, volunteers such as Winnie also provided hundreds of referrals, from where to get psychiatric care to information on drug rehabilitation. The center offered other services, too. Deaf Contact put hearing-impaired persons in touch with the hearing world via Teletype, and CheeRing provided regular telephone visits for people who were homebound. There was even a chapel in the office, where prayer requests could be remembered.

Over the years Winnie put in thousands of hours at Help Line, but those she helped never saw her, never met her, and didn't even know her full name. And that's the way she wanted it.

# A FRIENDLY LETTER

The pastor had given up trying to cheer Mr. Morgan. Crippled by age, defeated, and forgotten, the old gentleman spent most of his time at a rest home in Austin, Texas, grimly waiting to die.

But one day when the pastor dropped by to see him, Mr. Morgan was sitting up, smiling, and eager to talk. The remarkable change had been caused by a letter that had arrived that morning. It was the first letter he had received in twelve years.

The author of the letter was a thirteen-year-old schoolgirl named Nancy (not her real name). Writing letters was Nancy's special way of showing concern for lonely people such as Mr. Morgan.

"Actually, it was my grandmother who gave me the idea," she said. "Once when I went to visit her, she told me that my letters made her forget how lonely she was. She's lived alone ever since my grandfather died, but I had never thought of her as being lonely."

Nancy could not forget her grandmother's remark. She began wondering how many other lonely people could be helped by a friendly letter.

From churches and rest homes, Nancy collected names of elderly people who had no relatives or friends. Then she began writing to them. Most were confined to nursing homes, and for them she spun lively, humorous tales of her family and school.

Nancy soon had seventeen correspondents. One was a wealthy woman of seventy-eight who had lived by herself in haughty isolation for fifteen years. Before long she began to greet visitors with a disarming smile. "The day I saw Nancy's letter in the mailbox and realized the postman had not made a mistake," she recalled, "was the day I admitted to myself just how sour and shriveled my life had become. If someone Nancy's age thinks I'm worth writing to, well I guess it's not too late to start living again."

At least one of Nancy's correspondents began seeking out other lonely people and writing letters, too.

"Wouldn't it be marvelous," said Nancy, "if each person in the world would look for one lonely person to care about? But then there wouldn't be enough lonely people to go around."

—Story suggested by Linda Lee Hart

# "I CAN'T RESIST IT"

James D. Cannon, a custodian at Wirt High School in Gary, Indiana, was a large man with a rich, resonant voice and a deep belly laugh. Asked why, for fifteen years, he put so much of himself into sending greeting cards to strangers, he could hardly contain his enthusiasm for his cause of cheering people up.

"I do it because I can't resist it. I love people. It's my duty to be of help to the troubled and sick," he said. His wife, Olivia, helped send out the cards that brought warmth to thousands.

Jim had a varied career. Years earlier he was the star pitcher with the Steel City Giants. For a time he was a staff worker with a local neighborhood house; later he was a truck driver. Jim also taught Sunday school at St. Paul's Baptist Church for many years.

He found the people who needed cheering up through newspaper stories of accidents and from friends who let him know when anyone was ill or troubled. Jim didn't stop with just one card. He said, "I stick with them until they get out of the woods."

In response to his caring, a woman in Milwaukee, to whom he sent cards for months, cried, hugged, and kissed him when he drove there to visit her.

The mother of a young Virginia boy who lay paralyzed said that Jim's thoughtfulness did *her* even more good than it did her ill son by relieving some of her own anxiety.

A card dealer in Gary provided Jim with special cards for ten cents. His records show that Jim purchased 21,911 cards over a six-year period. With postage, that came to almost $4,000—and many hours, especially since Jim tried to include a little poem or message of his own on each one.

Cannon's hobby was rewarding—not only for the receiver of the greeting, but also for the sender. Jim said, "I wouldn't give up the chance to help these people for anything. Olivia and I find an inner reward that beats anything else we do."

—Reuben E. Olson

# A SECRET PEN PAL

When Linda Bremner's ten-year-old son, Andy, died of cancer, Linda was angry with God—and felt guilty about her anger. One day she came across Andy's address book, listing the names of twenty children he had met at a summer camp for cancer patients. The book reminded Linda of how much Andy had enjoyed receiving mail, and how he had been deluged with cards and letters while in the hospital but received none when he came home.

"I then became Andy's secret pen pal," Linda recalled. "I sent him greeting cards, funny stories, puzzles. I think he figured out who was sending them, but he never said a word, and neither did I."

Linda sat down, and to each child whose name was in Andy's book she wrote a chatty note. *Just twenty letters,* she thought.

But Linda had not bargained with her mail-starved recipients. "Thank you, thank you for your letter," the first boy wrote. "I never get any mail. I didn't think anybody even knew about me. I love you!"

Thus "Love Letters," a unique ministry to terminally and chronically ill children, was born. Before long, there were 620 children on Linda's list. Linda wrote each letter herself, and with the help of a volunteer staff and people who donated cards and trinkets, each youngster received a newsletter and another piece of mail (a postcard or small gift) once a month.

Linda sometimes worried about keeping Love Letters afloat, but she saw God's helping hand in everything. A small blurb in a Chicago newspaper led to an offer of an office—free. When her apartment was robbed of her one and only typewriter, a corporation donated a computer. And once, when a printer's bill of $139.25 was due, Linda received a notice from a bank about an inactive account. The account turned out to be one that she had opened for Andy when he was a baby, and later forgotten about. With interest, the account totaled $139.25.

"God healed me of all my anger," Linda said, "and he gave me a chance to bring comfort to children like Andy." Love Letters was certainly in good—and tender—hands.

—Joan Wester Anderson

# EYES TO SEE

At 4:00 P.M. every day, Raymond D. Flagg picked up the newspaper and wheeled himself over to the telephone.

"Hello, Mrs. Flower," he said, "are you ready for today's report? Well, first, there's the death of Hal Thompson, age seventy-three, of New Bedford. He's a lawyer. Did you know him? . . . I'm so sorry.

"There's a happy item about Mrs. John Owens. She had a baby boy."

And so it went. Ray Flagg was a news broadcaster with a unique audience, and one of the most appreciative: one blind person at a time. Every day from four until late in the evening, Flagg telephoned his blind clients to read them items from the local newspaper, the *New Bedford Standard-Times.*

He knew his clients only by voice: their ages ranged from fifty-eight to seventy-eight. There was no charge for Ray's services. He felt that what he did was its own reward. "This helps and cheers me as I hope it helps and cheers them too. What would I do if I were all alone?"

There was a time when he was. When his wife died, the world became an empty place for Ray. Overnight, the modest first-floor apartment in New Bedford—where the couple had lived for twenty-six years—became a painfully lonely place.

Ray had no alternative but to stay in the apartment. He was confined to a wheelchair. When he was a child, infantile paralysis had crippled his body but not his spirit.

One day something a friend said gave Ray the idea that helped fill the aching void left by his wife's death. "Blind people like to know what is in the daily newspaper but have no one to read it to them," the friend had remarked. So Ray began reading the paper to his blind friends—bringing the world closer to them and to himself.

Although he was an invalid, Ray was self-sufficient. He cooked his own meals and did his own housekeeping. A tiny pension supplied his needs. He was most grateful for that independence. "I don't need help. Thank God for that."

The man who was grateful to God for not needing help was equally grateful for the privilege of being able to help others.

—Manuel Almada

# TO BE OF USE

Billie Berry started her own fight against illiteracy in the world by teaching David (not his real name)—a thirty-two-year-old dyslexic master carpenter who graduated from high school without being able to read or write. But then, Billie Berry was *always* helping people.

"I was taught that the good Lord meant us to be of some use in the world," she said, "that one should use one's talents to help others."

Billie was the eldest of four children in a suburban Philadelphia family. During the Depression, Billie made herself useful as a social worker. Later she and her husband went to China, where they lived for seven years and where Billie taught English at mission schools.

In 1945, Billie's husband was killed in an auto accident in Singapore. Left with three small children to support, Billie decided to do it in a way that would be "of use." She set up a nursery school.

When it was discovered that she had cancer, Billie volunteered to work with the American Cancer Society, helping other cancer patients. And later, every Wednesday without fail, she was part of a team delivering Meals on Wheels to homebound people in the Newton, Pennsylvania, area.

And then there was David. Although the young man had a good vocabulary, he couldn't perform any of the basic reading and writing tasks. So Billie worked with him on syllabication. One day, after months of working together, Billie was reading David a newspaper story about three successful men who had been unable to read or write. She noticed that David's eyes were following the text.

"David," she said, "my voice is getting tired. Why don't you read to me for a while." And David found himself reading. He read, and read, and read. It was the very first time.

With the help of a bookkeeper friend, Billie designed personalized checks so that David could use them to practice writing. "My aim," Billie said, "is to teach David enough so that his little son will never know that 'once upon a time' his daddy could not have read even those simple words to him."

Billie saw nothing remarkable in her nonstop activities "to be of use." But when you consider all that she accomplished, it is *she* who was remarkable.

# PART OF A FAMILY

It all began the morning Betty Frazier read in the paper that a young woman had been confined to a local nursing home for lengthy therapy. The article said that the woman had few friends or relatives. Betty decided to pay her a visit.

And then she returned for another visit and another. Since Betty's children were grown, married, and living elsewhere, she had time to be neighborly.

In the nursing home, Betty observed that most of the other patients there were elderly people—men and women who, like herself, had become separated from their loved ones by time and distance. Each week as Betty walked along the corridors to her young friend's room, she couldn't help noticing their loneliness.

Gradually, these older patients came to recognize Betty. They would nod to her; some would whisper a greeting; others would just smile a bit, almost expectantly. With time, Betty found herself stopping along the way to her friend's room, chatting with the other patients. They clasped her hand with an eagerness that touched her heart. Before long, Betty's hour

47

with her friend expanded into afternoons with the other patients.

One day Betty went to the administrator of the nursing home with an idea. Then she went to the pastor of her church and got a list of all the parishioners. She telephoned each of them. Would they, she asked, be willing to "adopt" the elderly patients at the nursing home, remembering them at birthdays and holidays, sending them cards, even gifts, perhaps also visiting them occasionally? Practically everybody said yes.

That was how Project Reach Out came into being in Wellsboro, Pennsylvania. In a short time, other hospitals and nursing homes were asking Betty to find people to adopt their patients. Other pastors and their parishioners wanted to be part of her program.

It grew in depth as well as size. A man in his seventies, alone and an invalid most of his life, had been "adopted" by newlyweds who not only remembered him on important days and visited him in the hospital, but also frequently invited him to their home. The man said, "My adopted family has given me something I'd stopped believing ever existed: love."

For Betty Frazier and her "families," their reward was in their deeds, knowing that Jesus said, "When you do these things for others, you do them for me" (Matthew 25:40 paraphrase).

# THE BEST KIND OF GOOD NEIGHBOR

John Fling was the twelfth of the nineteen children in his family of Georgia sharecroppers. He grew up poor, but he always believed that there were people in greater need than he.

Hundreds of people in Columbia, South Carolina, thought of John as the best kind of good neighbor, for he spent some forty hours a week and much of the small salary he earned—as a parts-delivery man for an automobile dealer—lending a helping hand to the poor, the elderly, the disabled, and the children of his community.

The parents of two grown sons, John and his wife, Jane, had no telephone and no television. They had no car. They had owned three, but signed each of them over to families whose need was urgent and whose battered vehicles were beyond repair. Often John was able to use his company's truck to make his rounds.

John filled needs that organized groups didn't handle. He'd pick up a sick child at school, take an elderly man's terrier to the veterinarian (and pay the bill), arrange donations so a widow wouldn't lose her mobile home, even explain the difference between roach killer and window cleaner to a newly arrived Cambodian family.

A typical afternoon might have found John delivering fifty pounds of cat food to a ninety-one-year-old glaucoma victim's forty cats. He bought food for a woman unable to shop for herself and made a mental note to find her a working refrigerator.

John took special interest in blind people. He read mail to a blind couple and regularly took a group grocery shopping. "Who's going to make sure the blind don't become hermits?" he asked. He took them on trips to the mountains and beach, and even invented a couple of items to make life more fun for those without sight. One was a jogging pole, so they could exercise independently. The other, a go-cart equipped with walkie-talkies, allowed them to experience the thrill of racing around an open field. John provided the directions.

Each day John wore a cap with the words, "I love to tell the story" on it, the story of Jesus Christ's love for us. John's everyday deeds told that story, too.

—Penney V. Schwab

# "I LIKE TO SURPRISE PEOPLE"

Cheerful and smiling, Mary Konzek pedaled her blue bicycle all over downtown Sunnyside, Washington. Sometimes she was doing her own shopping, but most of the time she was out visiting lonely or needy neighbors, often with a small gift in her bike's wire basket. It might have been something she purchased ("I try to make the dollar stretch"), or one of the secondhand items she collected from friends. "I like to surprise people with a little food or something nice," Mary said. "But people don't need material things. They need company." Mary gave freely of both.

She visited six people regularly. Friends and relatives kept her posted about others who would benefit from her calls, but they said that Mary seemed intuitively to know when people were in need. And then she was quick to stop by.

Mary—who was "a good many years old"—never learned to drive a car. She had a lame leg, the result of childhood polio, but that did not stop her from "running around" on her bicycle. She learned to ride a bicycle at the same time her children did. "It took me a week, and my hands became so sore I could hardly hold a fork." For years Mary used a standard bike similar to the one on which she learned. "My children bought me a new model that's lightweight, but I can't get used to it. I still ride around on that old rattletrap."

Mary made a deliberate effort to do at least two good deeds daily.

"I can't expect anything in return," she said, "but I have been rewarded. I have my health, my five wonderful children, and sixteen grandchildren. It's like my favorite saying, 'Cast your bread onto the waters and it will come back with jelly on it!' "

Mary trusted God for strength to continue her goodwill visits. Her faith was deep, and deeper still after her successful battle with cancer.

Whenever Mary parked her bike at a new home, one of the first things she shared was a prayer. "I try to live by this prayer," she said: " 'May you live in the Spirit, that all who contact you will be strengthened, that all who bless you will be blessed, that all who give to you of love, money, or service, will be prospered; and if any should seek to injure you, may they contact your thought of God and be healed.' "

—Story suggested by Helen Driscoll

# LIKE THE PETALS OF A ROSE

One morning years ago I was jogging along West Shore Road in Conimicut, Rhode Island, when my attention was drawn to a gaunt older woman on the other side of the road. She was walking slowly, staring sullenly at the ground, her arms wrapped tightly around her thin body as if holding herself apart from the world. Deep, sad lines cut across her face. "She looked as though she'd lost her last friend," I said to my wife, Dorothy.

I found myself praying for the woman, wondering if I would meet her. *But what will I do if I meet her, Lord?* I prayed. *I mean, wouldn't it be too forward to walk up and start talking to her?* At once the thought came to me: *Smile at her.*

"No," I wanted to say. Smiling just isn't natural for me. *Smile,* the thought came again. Where had that thought come from? Was it from God?

It was weeks before I encountered the gaunt woman again. And when I did, her eyes stared straight ahead. But I looked eagerly in her direction and gave her a good smile. I don't think she even noticed. I felt deflated. But from somewhere deep within, a tiny voice seemed to prod me: *Don't give up.*

The next time I encountered the woman was a few days later. I found my smile and said cheerfully, "Good morning!" Again, nothing.

Again and again over the following weeks the encounter was repeated. "Hello!" "Good morning!" "Lovely day!" The words were always mine. The only other sounds were the roaring of the surf and the pounding of my running shoes. Could anyone enter this woman's sad, silent world?

*God, help me to reach her,* I prayed that night.

"Good morning! Lovely day!" I shouted on our next encounter. "Humpf!" she muttered, still staring stonily ahead.

But inside me, as I jogged on past, a kind of tension began to ease. *Praise God,* I thought. That "Humpf!" was like the opening of a door.

When I saw her again, she seemed different. Her arms were more relaxed and she was staring at me, her face puzzled.

"Good morning!" I shouted. "God bless you!" She nodded. And there—ever so faintly—wasn't that a smile tugging at her lips? Yes! Yes, it was! I felt a sense of accomplishment as I finished my jog that day.

The next time I saw her she was swinging her arms, head up, looking boldly toward me.

"G-good morning," I choked. "Morning," she replied softly, a timid smile on her lips.

When we passed a few days later, her "Morning" was followed by a soft "Th-thank you!" After that we met frequently, stopping to chat for a second or two, then longer. We had coffee, then several coffees. Her name was Pearl, and she needed someone to talk to. Slowly, like the petals of a rose, she opened her life to me. Her husband had died ten years earlier. Her two married sons had moved across the country. Friends had moved away too. She lived alone and felt abandoned, hurt, angry, bitter.

"Until you started smiling at me, I thought no one in the world could ever care about me again," she said. "So I told myself I didn't care either. I didn't need anybody!" She wiped her eyes. "But I learned from you what my wonderful husband had always tried to tell me: 'People really are nice, if you only give them a chance.' " She looked down.

I took Pearl home to meet Dorothy. They became friends too. We took her to church, where she began to make more friends. After that, when I jogged along West Shore Road, Pearl often flagged me down, saying, "I've been waiting for you! I have so much to tell you!"

All because of a smile.

—Don Vieweg

# FOR ALL OUR FRIENDS

Y ou might have walked up the path to the front door and started to ring the bell. But your hand would stop in midair. There was a sign by the doorbell:

> If no one answers when you ring,
> Don't turn and go away.
> Just wander through the garden gate
> And view the flowers gay.
> And as you wander, fancy-free
> Among the flowers there,
> Perhaps you'll want to bow your head
> And say a little prayer.

Intrigued, you would follow the directions until you came to the garden gate, where there was another verse:

> Our garden gate
> Doth open wide
> For all our friends
> To walk inside.

Overhead were the words: "The Lord's Garden."

Going through the gate, you would find yourself in an acre of blooms nodding in the sunshine. Behind the flowers was the entrancing background of the Rocky Mountains.

The gardener was Dr. August A. Hermann, a retired veterinarian. After coming back from the edge of death—from the first of several heart attacks—Dr. Hermann decided that God must have some special work for him to do. Since he and his wife loved to tend the garden in back of their Denver home, they decided to use its fruits to bless others.

Many friends, particularly grateful owners of pets, contributed plants for the garden. As people learned of it, they sent quantities of fine stock for testing, knowing that the blooms would serve a special purpose during the testing process. Eventually there were more than fifteen hundred rose bushes and three thousand lilies in the garden.

Each week for a period of several years, the Hermanns sent cut flowers to local hospitals. On Sundays they took flowers to nursing homes, and particularly fragrant blossoms went to the Home for the Adult Blind. On Easter Sunday they gave a potted plant to each of the one hundred Sunday school children in their church. For the church, Dr. Hermann constructed a styrofoam cross with glass tubes pressed into the surface for holding short-stemmed flowers.

Dr. Hermann was an elder of the North Presbyterian Church for twenty years and a member of a number of community organizations, including Rotary. Eventually, through Rotary's Jobs for Youth program, he hired a boy to help in the garden.

And so as you entered the garden you would be made welcome to enjoy the fragrance and beauty. You could not leave without carrying with you a bit of Dr. Hermann's spirit of selfless love for God, captured in a sign posted at the exit of the garden: "And I am his gardener."

—Josephone Robertson

# MARIE'S DISH GARDEN

Often when people around Palo Alto, California, found a cup without a handle or a chipped dinner plate in their china cabinet, they would not discard it. "Marie Green can use this," they would say.

Eighty-eight-year-old Marie Green, as her name could suggest, was partial to growing things, and her specialty was the "dish garden." She took those handleless cups and chipped plates, and into them went a little potting soil, a few small rootings—cacti, fern, spider plants. Then she added some decorative pebbles and—presto! The ugly, broken items had been transformed into vessels of beauty.

When Marie had readied a dozen or so dish gardens, she donated them to groups which, in turn, offered them for sale at modest prices. All proceeds went toward scholarships or missionary programs at Marie's church, First United Methodist.

Marie always sent along personal instructions with her plantings: "Place in a sunny window." "Keep soil moist." "Feed one tablespoon of plant food occasionally." And she let it be known that she was available for consultation if a problem arose.

As a small girl on a farm in Oklahoma, Marie knew she had the gift of a green thumb. Back then, she successfully raised produce for sale. "How well I remember the beautiful blue velvet coat I bought with the money," she said.

After moving to Palo Alto with her husband and small son in 1937, Marie, who had earned a teaching degree, designed and taught the first elementary school science classes. But even after retirement, she was still a teacher. For three hours each week she volunteered to instruct senior citizens and third-grade children in the art of gardening. Each child worked with an adult; side by side, they planted and cultivated both vegetables and flowers.

The care and feeding of plants was not Marie's only concern. One day a week she helped out at an ecumenical Food Closet, where she served food to the needy. "We give them more than food," Marie said. "We give them hope."

"Marie's dish gardens," a church member said recently, "are perfect for the elderly who cannot move about easily or who live in small spaces." Looking at what would have been discarded and seeing new life growing in it—that's hope too!

—Kay F. Anderson

# A LILY IN THE DEBRIS

It was Eastertime in Okinawa, 1945. All was desolation and ugliness. Suddenly, a shell burst in front of Chief Carpenter's Mate George Walker, exposing a delicate pink lily in the debris. It seemed like a gift of beauty, a gift of life in the midst of death.

He stooped and dug up the plant, thrusting it into the pocket of his jacket.

The next spring, back home in Los Angeles, California, civilian Walker came across the forgotten, withered remains of the lily in his old jacket. Hopefully, he planted the bulb. It grew.

At Easter it bloomed again. The flower with a white cross at its center and golden stamens formed a star. To George Walker, it was a symbol of eternal life.

One day George overhead a Gold Star mother exclaim in grief, "If only I had some little keepsake from Okinawa to remind me of him; I have no grave to visit, to decorate. . . ."

George had wondered about the lily: How had this plant, native to South America, come to Okinawa? He never found out, but now he felt there was a reason for it. He believed he had a God-given mission to share the lily with others.

He waited until his lily produced another bulb, and then presented it to a Gold Star mother. When her bulb multiplied, she in turn was to present the new plant to some other bereaved mother.

At one point, George estimated he had given away more than three thousand Gold Star lilies.

"I can't always fill requests," he said. "The job is too big for me, but how do you stop kindness?"

Mothers wrote to him, telling how their bulb bloomed on a son's birthday or a cherished anniversary. They sent poems about the lily. One woman in Lubbock, Texas, wrote after her house had caught fire. In her excitement, she had thrown the pot with the lily out the window. The house burned to the ground. Three days later, as she stood by the blackened ruins, she saw—near the edge of the ashes—the Gold Star lily. It was blooming.

"It gave me strength to go on," she wrote.

And so the lily and George Walker, the man who found beauty on a desolate Okinawa beach, continued to bring a message of hope and consolation to the bereft.

—Story suggested by Rose H. Anderson

# THE ROSE MAN

**H**ello. Do you like roses?" The smiling man at the
door was slight of build, almost fragile, with thinning silver
hair.

"Yes, I do."

"Then here's one for you. I'm the Rose Man."

I had heard of this fabled man. For thirty years, he and his
wife, Ellen, had been visiting Broward General Hospital in Fort
Lauderdale, Florida, leaving roses with patients. Then one day
they came to my own hospital room, and I learned firsthand
about their quiet ministry to the sick.

Anthony "Nick" Nichols, eighty-five, and his wife, eighty-
one, cultivated more than six hundred rose bushes in the
backyard of their modest home. Twice a week they selected,
clipped, and dethorned about fifty long-stemmed roses to take
to patients. Before entering each room, they prayed that they
could show God's love.

"A single rose isn't much," Nick admitted, "but it shows we
care. And it gives us an opening—sometimes only for a word
of cheer or a breath of prayer, but many times God leads us to

deeper involvement." Once, in answer to Nick's, "Why are you here?" a lad murmured, "I'm just tired of running. I tried to commit suicide." Nick listened, and then shared God's love and concern. On leaving, he gently asked, "When are you going to stop running, son, and let God take over your life?" And as Nick put it, "Right then I shared in the joy of seeing another soul fall in love with Jesus and find a purpose for living."

Nick had been telling people about God and leading them into his kingdom for almost sixty years—since returning from World War I severely wounded. An upbeat thinker, he declared that the wartime explosion that almost took his life had led to his spiritual conversion—and to his disability pay, which enabled him to spend more time telling others about Jesus.

As a young man he had been a portrait artist and sculptor; but his joy became watching God mold lives. Besides the roses, he wrote twenty to thirty birthday notes daily, enclosing spiritual messages. (One year he mailed more than seven thousand.) Each time he read or heard of a young person who had been honored or who was in trouble, he tried to obtain their birthdate and add them to his file. Nick helped hundreds of young people through those epistles of joy.

"It's wonderful how God provides," Ellen said. "Every time the financial need grows beyond Nick's disability pay and social security, God sends aid. We've come to expect this—like the stranger who volunteered to pay for all our tracts, hundreds of dollars worth each year."

Once, when local residents learned "The Rose Man" himself was hospitalized, they deluged this gentle man with more than 2,300 get-well cards and roses.

—Grace Chavis

# FLOATING WITH GOD

In the shallow end of the YMCA swimming pool in Winston-Salem, North Carolina, a woman floated on her back. Her face was etched with fear, her jaws locked with tension. Standing beside her in the pool was her instructor, Whit East, who repeated, "Just relax. I'm right here beside you. I won't let you sink."

Whit East's desire to help people feel at home in the water began at the age of eight, right after he learned to swim. By age fifteen he had earned his senior lifesaving certificate, and a short time later he joined the YMCA as swimming coach and aquatic director.

Then came World War II. Whit was stationed in England with the U.S. Army. He visited a military hospital, where he saw wounded men being put into a swimming pool for therapy. "It gave me an idea," he recalled. "I decided that when I got home, in addition to regular swimming lessons, I'd use my aquatic talents to teach people how to overcome their disabilities."

Back in Winston-Salem, Whit rejoined the YMCA staff and spent his free time at the swimming pool, often teaching disabled persons. After fifty years of service, he retired.

Whit soon began working with a group of about twenty men and three women who had experienced strokes, back problems, knee and hip replacements, or brain damage.

As word of his classes got around, doctors began sending their patients to Whit, telling him what type of therapy to implement and helping him devise programs to suit individual needs. Depending on their abilities, Whit would have a person walk through the water, do arm and leg exercises, use a kickboard and aquatic dumbbells, tread water, float, or swim.

In addition to regaining the use and control of their bodies, many in Whit's classes found that the water helped them work out their anger and frustration about their physical limitations. "I show them how the water offers support as well as resistance," Whit says. "Life does too. If you can learn to use support and resistance creatively, you can be an overcomer."

Whit East found his own support through prayer and by "floating with God." He said that God gave him his talent, "so I stay close to him and pass that talent on."

—Allene Robinson

# "TOTAL NONSENSE"

Twelve years ago a heart attack and a series of strokes forced Edgar Dodenhoff to give up his jobs as a high school teacher and an electrician.

"He's totally disabled," said his doctors.

"That's total nonsense," said his wife, Edith.

She put a CB radio on a card table next to his bed; a neighbor put an antenna on a tree—and Edgar, clicking around the CB channels, started to pick up distress calls from boaters on the lower Delaware Bay, which was about three miles from his house in Frederica, Delaware.

Edgar came to the aid of thousands of lost or imperiled boaters by acting as a link between vessels in trouble and the people who could help—all the while being confined to a wheelchair in his home.

Early on, Edgar had discovered that boaters in trouble often couldn't make radio contact with the Coast Guard or other marine rescue services. Operators on land often didn't know how to pinpoint the caller's location or make contact with the proper rescuers. Edgar did know:

66

for years before his illness he had been captain of a forty-foot boat.

As Edgar started rousing marine rescue operations and directing them to floundering crafts, the Coast Guard quickly recognized Edgar's contributions. At their request he installed more powerful antennas and radios in order to cover all of Delaware Bay. He also became a member of the Coast Guard Auxiliary, answering about three hundred distress calls a year. In addition, he volunteered his communications skills to a wildlife-protection agency.

Working from his wheelchair, Edgar operated what is called Radio Station High Point, monitoring messages from six hundred square miles of water.

In the mid-1980s, Edgar's own life was saved. While talking to the Marine Police about a tow for a fishing boat with engine trouble, he suffered a sudden heart attack. The police had an ambulance rushed to his house.

Edgar doubts that he would have survived if he hadn't been in contact with the police at the moment of the attack. The fact that his life was saved because he was helping others merely confirms two of his philosophies: "What you give to life, you get back," he says. "And the good Lord watches over all of us."

# TOUCHING WORDS

That's the way Braille dots are arranged to spell the word *caring*, and caring is a good way to describe the thousands of men and women who volunteer their time to transcribe manuscripts into Braille so that the blind can "read" with their fingers.

One of these caring people was Virginia Fischer, who lived in Okemos, next door to Michigan's state capital of Lansing. Virginia's interest in Braille began when her daughter's college roommate, who was blind, visited the family on weekends. Later, she happened to read in a local newspaper that a class in Brailling was being organized. It was described as "a new hobby." Virginia signed up.

During her nine-month course, Virginia discovered that the Braille alphabet consists of varying combinations of one or more raised dots in a six-dot oblong known as the Braille cell. One page of conventional printing equals two or more pages in Braille—so an average-length book becomes two or three volumes in Braille. The Bible alone requires twenty Braille volumes!

After learning to use a typewriterlike machine called a Perkins Brailler, Virginia spent the last month of her course preparing a trial manuscript—thirty-five pages of solid, accurate Braille—to submit to the Library of Congress. As a result of her successful effort, she was certified by that library as a transcriber of literary works. The Brailling of math and science text calls for separate certifications, and Virginia also worked toward those.

Sitting at the Perkins Brailler that her husband helped set up in their sunny den, she was often supervised by her two cats as she put in an average of four hours each day on her unusual hobby. In addition to accepting assignments to do Braille books for the state library for the blind and for local students, Virginia filled individual requests for Christmas cards, church programs, and Masses. And some restaurants in the area requested menus in Braille.

"Once," said Virginia, "I read an item about how thrilling it is for a blind person to be able to read Braille—like touching words and having them touch you back. There's an excitement to it that a sighted person doesn't know."

But because of her caring work as a volunteer, Virginia is among the very special sighted people who *do* know.

—Margaret Gunn

# THE SPECIAL ONES

The sounds of sirens and horns on the road around Aurora, Illinois, announced the approach of Kelley's Korral—a wooden wagon with bright yellow trim pulled by a two-mule team. Inside, each of the special passengers was delightedly pulling the cord of a siren or air horn.

Mr. V. A. Kelley, a bespectacled, pleasant-faced, fifty-eight-year-old carpenter, was at the reins of the wagon, which he built himself. He took mentally challenged children and adults for free rides, in the hope of bringing a little pleasure into their lives.

He called those children "the special ones." Kelley originally conceived the idea of the mules and wagon for his grandson, who was "special."

"The passengers come from schools for those with mental or physical disabilities," his wife, Alice, reported. "The wagon holds twelve children and an aide to care for them."

Kelley, who was raised on an Illinois farm and spent twenty-four years in the feed and grain business, traced his need to help the disabled to his childhood. "As a boy on the farm, I used to watch my mother care for the eggs in the incubator. The stronger chicks would pick a hole in the shell and hatch out healthy. Others were so weak my mother had to help them out. Those she gave to me, and with special care, even the weak would improve."

Kelley believed that the key to providing some happiness was in helping the children "get out of their shells."

His project was part of a long history of caring for unfortunate children. In 1953 he visited Korea and was greatly moved by the plight of biracial orphans. He and his wife, who already had one daughter, adopted a young Korean brother and sister, and Kelley worked to find American homes for forty-five other children.

It was Kelley's dream someday to have a trailer big enough to transport both wagon and mules. "I'd like to be able to reach children in other communities," he said. "When a shy, withdrawn child timidly pets one of the mules and you see the child's joy, you just want to do more."

# SONGS BY THE DEAF

The morning hymn filled the Forest Park Baptist Church in Joplin, Missouri. But the people in the first two pews didn't make a sound. Instead, they intently watched the young woman who stood facing them, their arms and hands moving in perfect unison as she led them in the sign language of the deaf.

That was just one of the numerous services that Kathleen McCoy Ramseyer performed in her years of volunteer work as interpreter to the deaf. She even taught her mother, Olga McCoy, the sign language so that she could help out when needed. Together with her mother, Kathleen operated a thriving nursery and flower shop, but countless hours were spent with their deaf friends. Both Kathleen and her mother had perfect hearing.

Kathleen first learned sign language from her roommate at college. Eventually she gave up her lifetime dream of being a missionary in India to devote herself to helping deaf persons.

"I had a sudden feeling," she said, "that God put me in Joplin because he wanted me there."

An average day would find Kathleen making hospital calls to explain deaf patients' needs in emergency situations, or visiting homes where a deaf child could not make himself understood to his parents—who had not yet mastered sign language. Both Kathleen and her mother appeared in court to interpret for the deaf.

Every Sunday Kathleen and her mother drove some of their deaf friends to church, where Kathleen interpreted the morning services for them. They had their own choir and sometimes "sang" for the congregations, with beautiful sign-renditions of well-known hymns.

"It is sad that the deaf have so much difficulty in communicating with people around them," Kathleen said. "But in our Bible-study and prayer group, I have the distinct feeling that they communicate easier with God than many of us who hear. In their silent world, his 'still, small voice' speaks without noisy interference."

—Story suggested by Jorunn Rickets

# A BIKE FOR JERRY

Bud Lee, a retired Montana farmer, often walked past the house in Denton where his young neighbor Jerry Clark lived. There he could see the three-year-old boy sitting by the window in his wheelchair, watching children play. Jerry was paralyzed from the waist down from a birth injury, and Bud could tell by the look on the boy's face how much he longed to be outside with the other children.

Then one day Jerry's mother, Barbara Clark, brought Bud a picture of an antique hand-operated bicycle she had found in a magazine. "It's just the thing for Jerry," she said, "but it's no longer being manufactured. Do you think you could build one of these?" Bud was not surprised by her request, and he said he would certainly try.

Shortly after his retirement, Bud had set up a small repair shop. "It was just a place to tinker," he said, but soon folks began saying that Bud could build anything.

However, Jerry's bike was a big undertaking. Bud had no blueprints. Every step was trial and error. He bought a few parts and salvaged other parts from old bicycles. Yet gradually, with a great deal of ingenuity and care, Bud built a unique, chain-driven, hand-powered, three-wheeled bike.

When it was all done, the Clarks were delighted—especially Jerry. And before long Bud was getting orders from parents of other children with physical disabilities. Soon he had built more than twenty of his special bikes, taking about two weeks to construct each one. Three went to Shriner Hospitals for Crippled Children; others went to children in Montana and eight other states. One was used by the little girl who was Montana's March of Dimes poster child. And when Jerry grew too big for his bike, Bud built him a larger one.

Bud would not accept a cent for his work. For a long time he bought all the parts himself; then he would get an occasional donation from the nearby Lewistown Shriners Club, of which he was a member. And when people tried to pay him, his response was similar to what he told the Clarks: "The look on Jerry's face as he rides down the sidewalk is all the payment I need."

—Roberta Donovan

# SPECIAL DELIVERY

Delivery boys are now a thing of the past, but at one time they came in all shapes and sizes—as well as with a variety of speeds and attitudes. Some came to the door like beleaguered deliverers of doom, while others came on the bound, as though there were more rewards to work than the pay.

David Ward, of Memphis, Tennessee, was the latter kind. Weekdays after school and Saturdays, David pedaled his bike for the Speedway Drug Store. And David was good at his job. When he delivered a prescription and said, "I hope you're feeling better" in that polite, concerned way of his, somehow you did feel better.

One year, on a Saturday night before Christmas—David, who was then thirteen—received his usual salary for the week. But he did not go home. He had a special delivery of his own to make.

First he went down to the lot where the Christmas trees were being sold. When he had given a number of the trees his careful inspection, he bought one and loaded it on his bicycle. Then he wheeled it over to 605 Life Street, the home of a steady customer, Mrs. Brady Neals. She was seventy-one. And she had been blind for thirty-seven years.

"It's me, Mrs. Neals, David from Speedway," he said when she came to the door. Then David walked in, set up the tree, and talked cheerily as he trimmed it with the lights and decorations he had brought along.

Mrs. Neals could hardly speak. Even as David was leaving, she could only mumble her thanks. But she was thrilled. She kept reaching out to touch the tree's branches and to breathe its forest-fresh fragrance. "I'm seventy-one years old," she kept saying over and over, "I'm seventy-one years old and I've never had a tree."

Delivery boys used to come in all shapes and sizes—and some of them brought more to their jobs than work.

—Jack Martin

# SUCH A SMALL THING

Once a week a dignified, middle-aged mother left her home in Newton Square, Pennsylvania, with packages under her arm and drove to the Delaware County Women's Prison. Hours later, she returned without the packages. Was Mrs. Sarah Brock up to something sinister?

Not at all. Sarah, an amateur artist and needlework expert, was teaching inmates how to sew, knit, and do other handwork. Her hobbies became a bright spot for dozens of women in prison. She also provided material and supplies begged from friends, stores, manufacturers, and church groups.

Sarah began her prison class after deciding that there must be something she could do to help. Because the class was noncompulsory, only a few women showed up at first. But when other inmates saw their beautiful work, how they were able to decorate their drab cells with colorful pillows, stuffed animals, and other decorations, *they* became interested as well. Some even sold their work to earn money.

"These women still want to be a part of the outside world. They love to make gifts for their families," said Sarah.

One teenage inmate, a girl named Frances, in prison for murder, was hostile at first. Then one night she sidled up to Sarah and asked, "Do you think I could do something?"

Maybe it was the extra attention Sarah gave to Frances; maybe it was her sense of achievement when she finished a colorful elephant toy for her bed. Whatever it was, her attitude changed. Later, paroled and in a foster home, she became a useful and happy young woman.

There is another reason for the success of Sarah's involvement. The inmates knew she was there, working without a salary, because she wanted to be—because she really cared.

"It's such a small thing to share a hobby," Sarah said. "So many prisoners—men as well as women—never had a chance to add any beauty to their world."

—Story suggested by Ann Scott Morningstar

# FREE HOUSES

In his workshop at his home in Hermosa Beach, California, amid wood shavings and the pungent smell of fresh paint, stocky Herb Besant, a former painting contractor, designed and built houses to give away.

They were birdhouses, and making them became an unusual community service as well as a hobby for Mr. Besant. "After I retired, I found I had to keep busy," he related, "and one day I took some small scraps of wood in my workshop and made a few plain birdhouses. I painted them in bright colors, and when they were done, my wife asked if she could donate them for sale at her Woman's Club bazaar. They sold fast. So when our church was to hold a bazaar, I made some more, just a little more elaborate.

"My sister was in a rest home, and I took one to her to set it up on the patio where she could see it from her room. The nurses put feed out, and the birds came. You have no idea of the joy that the old people, who spend their entire day looking out a window, got out of that birdhouse and the birds that came to it.

"So I made some more for them, each one more elaborate. One I made like a castle, and I put a lamppost, complete with globe, on one corner. When the sun was setting each day, it would hit the birdhouse and make that lamp look like the light had just come on in it."

In the following years Herb made hundreds of birdhouses—Dutch farmhouses with windmills, intricate four-level Victorian mansions, Alpine chalets, Black Forest cottages—all of his own design and all given away to places where, he explained, "the most people could enjoy them."

"I don't know where I got the ability to create them," Herb said, "but I told my wife, Hazel, it must have come from our Lord."

When his talent became known around Hermosa Beach, Herb began getting offers from people who wanted to put him in business. "But at my age I don't want to make more money," he explained. "I just want to keep giving them all away, as long as I can."

# SOMETHING TO THINK ABOUT

Every Friday afternoon, when classes ended at Public School 189 on New York's Upper West Side, a group of fifth-graders hurried to Isabella House, a residence for elderly people. There they spent an hour listening to Fannie White as she told them all kinds of wonderful things about stamps. The children were around age eleven. Fannie was ninety-eight.

With each group, Fannie began her session talking about Benjamin Franklin, who started the U.S. postal system. "And how can you mention Franklin without touching on the American Revolution?" Fannie said. "The kids soon get the idea there's more to a stamp than its picture or the way to send a letter."

Through stamps, Fannie taught the children history (the lives of presidents and other famous people) and geography (about the countries and continents shown on the stamps). At the end of the hour, Fannie gave the youngsters some stamps for their own albums.

When Fannie moved into Isabella House, she brought along two big boxes of stamps that her nephews had given her when they went off to college. When she saw kids coming to be tutored by elderly volunteers, she knew that she, too, had something to offer. "So I got the school officials to alert their students," she said. "And that's how I started the Benjamin Franklin Student Stamp Club."

Fannie was also floor representative for her neighbors at Isabella House. Every day she saw to it that they got to the dining room, helped them with personal needs, and notified a nurse if they were sick.

Fannie was so lively that she would *bounce* out of a chair. How did she account for her physical and mental health? "My parents raised their five children with a firm sense of morality," she said. "We grew up in a little town in New Hampshire so free of stress that when we left, we took our tranquility with us."

After college Fannie became a social worker, then had a successful career in real estate. At age fifty-four she took up painting and had a one-woman show in a New York gallery. Her comfortable apartment in Isabella House was crowded with her paintings. One was a striking portrait of the philosopher Martin Buber, who inspired her when she heard him lecture. She read his chief work, *I and Thou*, in which Buber explored the direct personal relationship between human beings and God.

"That's a lot to think about," said Fannie. "And I'm still thinking."

—Sidney Fields

# LOOK UP TO THE LIGHT

Wherever he went, Leo Kremer was known as the "Kaleidoscope Man," and for good reason. Over the years he and his wife, Gerry, made an estimated ten thousand kaleidoscopes—and gave them all away.

Following the directions printed in an old issue of *Popular Science* magazine, Leo began his hobby using tubes from finished rolls of Teletype paper. At the time, he was a Teletype operator for the Union Pacific Railroad in Cheyenne, Wyoming. Later he switched to empty Pringles potato chip cans. He filled one end of the cans with multicolored glass, sequins, beads, and pieces of plastic that his wife had cut into bluebirds, hearts, rainbows, flowers, stars, and crosses.

At first Leo gave his custom-made kaleidoscopes to families in his church, then to the local veterans hospital, but his giving really took off by accident—quite literally. One day a car swerved off the road and knocked over the fence outside his home. The driver insisted on paying for the damage, but when Leo discovered she was a Catholic nun caring for sick children, he wouldn't hear of it. Instead, he showed her his kaleidoscopes. She immediately agreed that her kids would love them.

Since then, Leo's kaleidoscopes have entertained children in hospitals all over the United States and the world. One of his favorite stories was about a boy who had gone through an operation on his arm. Leo handed him a kaleidoscope and the boy immediately put it up to the light, exclaiming, "Look, a rainbow! A star!" At that moment the doctor walked into the room.

Taking Leo aside, the doctor said, "Thank you. We've been trying to get him to move his arm, but he just wouldn't. Your kaleidoscope did the trick."

A boy looking up to the light and taking new interest in life was the kind of unexpected gift Leo gave and received. At eighty years of age, he was still making kaleidoscopes. On each recycled potato chip can he wrote, "Give your talents and gifts to God, and he will do things with them that will surprise you."

—La Jeanne T. Gilmer

# PART OF THE FAMILY

One day Louise Montgomery was waiting for her car to be repaired in a small town in Maine. Into the auto shop strolled Alison Kelley, and the two women, who had never met, began chatting. Soon they discovered that though Louise was in her seventies and Alison in her fifties, they had much in common, especially the fact that both were strong believers in the power of prayer. Soon the two became prayer partners.

Alison, a registered nurse, often spoke to Louise about her volunteer work at a shelter for the homeless in Boston. "As we talked and prayed," Louise said, "I became convinced that God wanted me to try to open a shelter in Portland."

And so it happened that Louise and her husband, Claude, took their $50,000 life savings and began combing Portland for a big house. "You'll never find a house for that money," one real-estate agent told them.

But find one they did—a fourteen-room dilapidated structure. With help from the inmates of Cumberland County Jail, the Montgomerys restored the ceilings and floors, replaced broken windows, replastered, and painted. Claude, a noted artist, traded one of his paintings for appliances. Their daughter contributed a new furnace. Louise contacted every church in the area and obtained contributions of blankets, furniture, food, and money.

The night before one Christmas Eve, Friendship House opened its doors. It became home for hundreds of guests (sixteen at a time), without charge. Some were like Jenny, a woman in her fifties, who had been living in a boxcar under a bridge. One night during a blizzard she arrived at Friendship House, and stayed for the winter. Other people stayed anywhere from two weeks to two months. Most of them were helped to find a job and encouraged to save money for a new start.

Heidi came to the Montgomerys one day after roaming cross-country, trying to resolve her drug problems. "There was no space at the local rehab center," she reported, "and with the dirty clothes I was wearing, I wasn't welcome anywhere. But Friendship House opened its doors to me."

Former guests often returned, even after they were out and making it on their own—like David and Nancy Iarocci, who came back to manage the shelter and helped the Montgomerys begin a free day-camp for inner-city children.

"They know they are always welcome here," said Louise. "Some send donations. Sometimes they want to help out. But more than that, they come back because they feel part of the family."

—Cheri Fuller

# NO PLACE TO GO

There's doubtless no son or daughter who would refuse to take back into their home a mother who had been scarred but cured of cancer.

But mental illness? That's something else again.

A remarkable woman—Lula Mae Lazenby of Charlotte, North Carolina—had the dedication of a nun, the fire of an evangelist, and the understanding of an angel.

For years in the fifties and sixties, her home was open to patients released from hospitals for the mentally ill—women with no place to go. They had no place to go because families refused to accept them back into the circle—or because they feared to return.

It was just as well. Where there was no love, there could be no happiness. But in one home there was love.

"We're a family," said tall, smiling Lula Mae. She introduced her houseguests.

One woman in her fifties said she'd been in the hospital seventeen years before drugs made her well. There was nothing to suggest she'd ever been ill. She had lived with Lula Mae for two years.

The women talked about their year-round garden and how they took turns at household and kitchen chores. They told how they acted as hostesses and entertained when the Methodist Church Circle met in Lula Mae's house.

They also told of trips to the mountains, and to the church they attended with Lula Mae.

Lula Mae declared that her new family "made me young again, and anybody who thinks he's old at sixty-five needs to wake up. I'm more useful and happier now than I've ever been in my life."

When Lula Mae retired after fifty-one years as a dietician in the city schools, she prayed, "God, continue to use me. Please send someone into my home and life so that I can help them."

Lula Mae's prayer was answered. She had never been more needed or more useful in her life.

—Kays Gary

# ROOM AT THE INN

It was our first Christmas in America. We had left our parsonage in England so that our son and daughter might attend theological colleges in Washington and Missouri while we fulfilled some preaching engagements in the South.

After a service one evening in mid-December, a woman introduced herself. "This is not my church," she said, "but I feel that I have been wonderfully blessed tonight." And then she asked, "Where are you spending your Christmas?"

We did not know. Our children were to come to be with us, but where, we had no idea. "The Lord will make a way for us," we said.

It was then that the stranger offered her home to us for two weeks. She absolutely insisted that we accept.

And so we arrived at her lovely house just before Christmas. A huge "Welcome" sign greeted us with a note that read, "Everything is for your pleasure. Merry Christmas."

The marks of loving preparation were everywhere—in the Christmas tree and decorations, bowls of fruit and candy, and well-stocked cupboards. A turkey, an English plum pudding, and a ham were in the refrigerator. On Christmas morning there were gifts under the tree. All the while, our hostess was nowhere to be seen.

Once, after an afternoon of sightseeing, we returned to find a hot meal on the table. At other times, the refrigerator would be replenished while we were out.

But the best gift our unseen hostess gave was the love we felt everywhere. With rare insight, she had even sensed our need to be by ourselves for our Christmas reunion.

Just before we left she came to see us and explained that she had been staying in a garage apartment nearby. "After my husband died," she said, "my house seemed big and lonely. And so I have put it to use for God." We then discovered that our family was but one of many—including ministers, returning missionaries, and other servants of the Lord—whom she had sought out to help.

This woman's giving was the very essence of Christmas—for at her inn, there was room for strangers.

—Alice E. Duncombe

91

# A PLACE TO RECHARGE

Have you ever known a minister who needed a vacation? A pastor in desperate need of a place to get away from it all?

How about two weeks in a private home in a Florida beach town? That's what Hugh Hoffman had to offer, and the accommodations were absolutely free.

Hoffman came up with the idea of vacation homes for ministers when he was hospitalized for shell shock after World War II. Each day, as the chaplains made their rounds, Hoffman noticed how tired they looked and saw how little time they took off.

"Most of them never got much of an opportunity to take a vacation. And when they did, they didn't seem to have much money to go anywhere. That's when I felt that God called me to do what I'm doing," he said.

So Hoffman started Religious Vacations, Inc., by buying a three-bedroom home in Fort Lauderdale, Florida, not far from where he lived. Nine years later he added a second three-bedroom home to the project. Both houses were available year-round to any full-time ministers and their families, and both came furnished with linens, silverware, china, TVs in each bedroom—even popcorn poppers.

The newspaper arrived each morning on the front step, and there was a file box in the living room with listings of nearby restaurants, parks, pools, and tennis courts. The homes had everything—but a phone—for a perfect, uninterrupted holiday.

And the cost to the clergy? "Oh, I ask them to wash two or three windows and sweep the place out before they leave," Hoffman said. And if they still felt indebted, he would probably let them mow the lawn. Hoffman, a bachelor, also welcomed the occasional dinner invitation he would receive.

Home-cooked meals were not the only benefit to Hoffman. He heard many heartwarming stories from his guests about how the time off had helped them. Married couples, in particular, were grateful for the respite from the stress and long hours of ministry. "I've had some couples tell me that I might have saved their marriage," Hugh said.

Hoffman spent about twenty hours a week taking care of the houses and corresponding with ministers to make sure the houses were used. When he was not making arrangements for his guests, Hoffman ran a small accounting firm, but he made it clear that vacations were his vocation.

"I got called by God into operating vacation homes. When some tell me that they are leaving here recharged, then I know I'm doing just what God wants me to do."

# NO CHRISTMAS?

Long before most people would start thinking about Christmas, a woman named Edna Walker of Tampa, Florida, began an annual project that took months to finish and lasted until nearly the eleventh hour before Christmas.

Edna made doll clothing for dolls that the Salvation Army distributed to children who might otherwise go without a toy. She started making the tiny garments because, she said, "I wanted to return another's kindness."

The first year Edna sewed clothes for some fifty dolls. The next year she repeated the task. As the years went by, Edna dressed more and more dolls. One year, as she turned them over to the Salvation Army major, Edna said, "I don't suppose you really need these anymore. There isn't the poverty there used to be."

"Not need dolls?" The major sounded astonished. "Without them, many little girls would have no Christmas."

*No Christmas?* Edna thought back to a year when it had looked as if there would be no Christmas for her. It was 1916, and her father had been sick and without work. She understood

94

why her parents could not buy toys—but she was only six, and there had been a doll in the window of the store that had caught her eye.

Then, on Christmas Eve, a Salvation Army worker dressed in her blue uniform had come to their little house in North Carolina, bringing a big basket of food and goodies, and toys for each child in the family. For Edna there had been a lovely little doll dressed in hand-sewn clothes.

Edna loved that doll, dressed it, washed it, and slept with it. Never was there a doll that received more fond caresses than this one. Throughout the years, not a Christmas has passed but what Edna remembered that shining moment of joy made possible by another's kindness.

As she remembered, Edna's fingers seemed to glide a little faster over the material she was molding into another doll outfit—an outfit she hoped would make some little girl just as happy as she had been on that special Christmas long ago.

—Story suggested by Mildred H. Comfort
and Nancy MacRoberts

# JAY DAY

In the mid-1980s, Dr. Robert Silverman temporarily closed his dental practice in Cleona, Pennsylvania, and took his family to Iowa City, Iowa. His five-year-old son, Jason, had leukemia, and the University of Iowa Hospital was one of the few places in the nation where the boy could receive a bone marrow transplant.

One day when shopping in Iowa City, Dr. Silverman came upon a contribution box with Jason's picture on it. People he didn't know, total strangers, had started a fund-raising campaign for Jason. They also loaned the family a house, supplied furnishings for it, and even provided a car for trips to the hospital.

The bone marrow transplant was successful, but three months later, with a weakened immune system, Jason contracted measles and died. In spite of his grief, Dr. Silverman never forgot the kindness of those who had helped them.

He spearheaded a program that organized groups to provide for the needs of leukemia patients' families while they were away from home. He joined a county organization for the mentally challenged and sponsored a youth baseball team. And for several years he led a dental team to Central America, supplying free dentistry to people in remote areas.

But of all Dr. Silverman's activities, the one closest to his heart was what he called "Jay Day." Each September 5, Jason's birthday, he would treat anyone needing dental care—on a no-cost basis. The first year, with the assistance of one hygienist, he treated seventy people. The next year, with the help of another dentist and a dozen volunteers, one hundred people were treated by closing time.

After the last patient had left, Dr. Silverman removed his rubber gloves and smiled. When asked if he would do it again, he said, "If I did it a hundred times, it wouldn't begin to repay the kindness others have shown me."

—Janet Rhine

# GOD'S GRACE AND A GOOD IDEA

At one time, at a hundred and seventy campuses across the country, hundreds of students were attending college thanks to Chicago businessman Swede Roskam. Were it not for his ingenuity, the students would not have had their scholarships.

In the mid-1940s, Swede graduated from high school with a burning desire to go to college, but he had no money to pay for it. Instead, he took a factory job in his hometown of Waterloo, Iowa. Then, during the summer, a college admissions officer who knew of Swede's ambition asked him to visit an elderly farming couple in Iowa. They had recently lost their son in World War II and wanted to do something for a boy their son's age.

That afternoon spent in the couple's farmhouse changed Swede's life. After he went home, they called the college and offered to fund Swede's entire education—"every detail," he recalled, "down to my class ring."

Swede went on to graduate school and embarked on a highly successful career as a salesman, marketing industrial products.

He married, raised five children, and sent them to college, always hoping that he could help other kids too.

In 1982, Swede founded Educational Assistance Ltd., a nonprofit organization working on the age-old principle of bartering. Swede arranged for corporations to donate excess inventory to EAL. The goods were in turn donated to colleges. The colleges responded by offering scholarships to needy students sponsored by EAL. It is what a salesman like Swede might call a win-win proposition. Companies won tax deductions, colleges won needed supplies, and students won educations. In ten years, EAL raised several million dollars in scholarships and helped more than a thousand students.

Eventually, Swede would still spend several months a year on the road as a salesman for Oil-Dri Corporation, but half the time he volunteered for EAL, finding ways the haves could help the have-nots. "By the grace of God, I was able to go to college and have the career I've had," he said. By God's grace and a good idea, he made sure others would follow.

# SPARKY'S GARDEN

At the far end of the grounds of a California mental hospital, there was an English walnut tree lending shade to a tiny garden. A sign posted on the tree trunk proclaimed "Sparky's Garden of Encouragement" and invited the passers-by to sit down, rest, and chat over a cup of Sparky's coffee. Almost every day, Sparky, the lord of that little realm, rode a bus to the institution to preside at his coffee table and dispense his own brand of friendship and cheer.

Most of his visitors were hospital patients. He gave them encouragement, urging them to trust and cooperate with their doctors.

"Do discouraged people come here very much?" I asked him one day.

"Every day," he said. His dark eyes danced as he spoke. "I talk to them and try to give them back some of the things they have lost."

"Lost?"

"Yes. Maybe they've lost faith in themselves, in God, in everybody about them. Many believe they're forgotten in the

100

'port of missing ships,' and I tell them that somebody is sure to remember. I give them a nice cup of hot coffee and a good magazine to read, and invite them to come back."

"And do they come back?" I asked.

"Sure they do. Sometimes there are questions they want to have answered. I answer them if I can. And then I let them work in my garden." He gestured with pride to the plot of ground where radishes, tomatoes, and lettuce were thriving in orderly array.

"There were four women patients here whom the doctor said couldn't be helped. I put them to work in my garden last summer. Three improved so much that they have gone home. The fourth could have gone, but she had no home to go to. They just needed a little help to get their thoughts untangled."

Small and wiry, with a contagious smile, Sparky talked and walked in rapid-fire fashion, but there was tranquility in his nature. To support himself and his garden, he washed cars and did odd jobs. The bulk of his free time went to his "Garden of Encouragement."

Why did he do it? Because of his gratitude and concern. At one time, Sparky was a patient in the hospital himself.

—Asa Z. Hall, M.D.

# THE SUNSHINE BOYS

When Andy Frederickson lost his wife to cancer, he knew he had to find some way out of the loneliness he felt. Then he remembered that when he had visited his wife in the nursing home during her final days, he had seen a beauty salon for the women, but the men seemed to be in constant need of haircuts.

Andy was a retired barber, so he decided to volunteer his services at the home. His only problem was how to get there. Blinded by cataracts, Andy could no longer drive a car. His lifelong friend, Harry Drew, agreed to chauffeur him.

Every Tuesday morning at 9:30 sharp, the two men would drive to Trementon's Box Elder County Nursing Home. Once there, Harry started rounding up the men who needed haircuts and ushering them to the temporary barber chair and an expectant Andy. While Andy clipped, Harry stood with dustpan and broom at the ready to sweep up the snippets.

Once the haircutting session was over, the two men would make the rounds of the home, pausing to chat with each resident. Then off they would go to the adjoining Bear River

Valley Hospital for some more haircutting and friendly chatter. Little wonder that eighty-four-year-old Andy and eighty-eight-year-old Harry were known as "The Sunshine Boys."

How did a man who couldn't see well enough to drive a car cut a head of hair? Well, Andy said he did it "by feel." And, he laughingly added, "I haven't cut anybody's ear off yet."

—Jody Jensen

# A Friend to the Lonely

Marie Carrano, a short, lively woman with expressive dark eyes, had two careers. By day she was the one-woman clerk, cashier, and supervisor at the Tastee Thrift Bread Box in New York City's north Bronx. There she served her customers—most of whom were poor or elderly, living on limited incomes—as they bought day-old bread, cakes, and pies.

Marie's other job began at night, after she returned to her tenement flat in the south Bronx, where she had been born long before it became a ghetto of burned-out buildings and treeless streets.

One evening Marie happened to read a newspaper story about an elderly woman in a small New England town who had never in her life received a letter. Marie sent her one. Back came a grateful reply, and a request: Would Marie please write to a lonely neighbor down the road?

"After that I started writing to other lonely people," Marie said. "I don't know how many now." She guessed it to be more than seven hundred—young and old, widows, widowers, singles, couples, people of all faiths. Some were ill; some were in need; some needed only a prayer or a warm word, even if it came from an unseen stranger. Some put stamps in their letters to make sure she would write again.

Marie was a collector, too. Neighbors and janitors notified her when a family was about to move from the area. She hurried over to collect what they didn't want: clothes, books, bits of costume jewelry, even old eyeglasses. She cleaned everything, packed the stuff in cartons, and sent it to her correspondents. "It makes nice birthday and anniversary presents," Marie said.

At home, on top of a secondhand desk, Marie had ten metal file boxes containing five-by-seven-inch cards with the names, addresses, birthdays, anniversaries, hobbies, and other essential information about her unseen friends.

Since she couldn't afford to purchase birthday or anniversary cards, Marie made her own. She cut out flower patterns from discarded fabrics and pasted them onto blank paper with her own well wishes. "I think my friends like them more because of the personal touch," Marie said. "Real handmade."

Marie Carrano may live in a world of secondhand clothes and day-old bread, but there's nothing secondhand or day-old in the quality of her friendship.

—Sidney Fields

# "LET'S GO!"

A thin, white-haired elderly man waited anxiously on his porch until the white sedan suddenly came into view; then his wrinkled face broke into a smile.

Keith Sewell had arrived to take him for a drive—the only outing the old man ever got to take. Soon three other older men joined him in the car, and they drove off for an afternoon of fishing and companionship. Keith, a dark-haired, forty-year-old bachelor, was a Memphis, Tennessee, plumber who spent weekends helping senior citizens cope with monotony and loneliness.

Perhaps it was because of his own speech and hearing defects, which made him more aware of the disabilities of others, that Sewell began his outings for oldsters. As he drove around town answering calls for plumbing jobs, he noticed many older men sitting listlessly on their porches. He wanted to provide some kind of recreation for them.

"Most of them live on fixed incomes and have no funds or way of getting around," he said. Sewell learned of men whom he might help through his work at the nursing home where he

106

visited his grandmother and the First Seventh-Day Adventist Church where he was a member.

Keith shared his love of the woods and nature by conducting drives and walks in the country, and berry-picking and fishing expeditions. In inclement weather, he often took his friends bowling.

"One time," Keith recalled, "we were going blackberry picking, and it started to rain. I thought we'd have to cancel the trip, but my elderly friends threw on raincoats and said, 'Let's go.'"

Sewell also visited senior-citizen shut-ins and did odd jobs around the homes of those who couldn't do them themselves. He tried to be helpful to the elderly whenever he could, but mainly he wanted to put some enjoyment into their lives and give them something to look forward to.

"It's wonderful to see them doing things," he said. "You can see in their faces the joy they get in going somewhere."

# "YOU CAN FIX ANYTHING"

When my husband, Howard, was only sixty years old, he was forced to accept early retirement from his job as a successful sales manager. He immediately started job-hunting. I was a nurse at Mur-Ci Homes, which housed twenty-four youngsters with severe disabilities in Nashville, Tennessee. They spent their waking hours in wheelchairs that were badly in need of repair.

"Howard," I pleaded one day, "you can fix almost anything. Why not volunteer to fix the wheelchairs at Mur-Ci? A new one costs over $600, and Mur-Ci hasn't got the money."

"I'm still job-hunting," he said.

But he wasn't having much success, and he was getting increasingly restless. I finally persuaded him to come to Mur-Ci to meet Billy, a ten-year-old hydrocephalic, who could not talk or sit up straight because of a spinal curvature. His wheelchair had no supports, a foot rest was broken, and the tray was held together by a shredded strap. On the drive home, Howard told me everything he would need to rebuild the wheelchair.

"Where would you get all that?"

"We'll know after we pray," he said.

We prayed that night. Early the next morning, Howard drove off. He returned in the afternoon with a carload of lumber, vinyl, Formica, slabs, and foam rubber. "Donations from friends in the building business," he explained, and turned to set up a shop in the garage.

Two days later he brought the rebuilt, handcrafted chair to Billy, who sat in it—erect, head up and comfortable against the padded supports, his feet firm on a foot rest. Howard showed him how the new tray could slide in and out. Billy propped his elbows on the tray, strained to bring his hands together, and strained even harder to clap three times.

"That's the most wonderful thanks I'll ever hear in my life," Howard exclaimed, his eyes glowing. He looked around at the other children in their shaky wheelchairs. "Who's next?" he asked.

From then on, he spent up to ten hours a day modifying, improving, and rebuilding wheelchairs. He persuaded suppliers to donate the necessary materials, and he built each new chair to fit the physical needs of each child, consulting orthopedists and therapists for advice.

Howard continued his wheelchair work until a sudden flurry of funds allowed Mur-Ci to buy new ones. I wondered if he would go back to sales, but before I could even ask, he was volunteering his skills to Civitan, a group that helps adults with mental disabilities!

—Joanna Long

# "FIX-IT" MANN

Jethro Mann ran a lending library. Not a library with a circulation desk, shelves of books, and constant reminders not to talk above a whisper. No, his borrowers traded shoptalk in loud voices about wheels, brakes, handlebars, and spokes. And though they arrived empty-handed on foot, they left on two wheels—bicycle wheels. Jethro Mann ran a lending library of bikes.

He retired from his job as an inspector for the North Carolina Department of Labor, but he had always been handy at fixing things. In fact, that was part of what he had been doing since someone gave him a few old, dilapidated bikes. The brakes didn't work, the handlebars were broken, the seats were rusty, and sometimes spokes were missing.

"Maybe you can find some use for them," his friend suggested. Mann did. He reconstructed a bike for himself, the first he had ever owned—at the age of sixty-three.

That gave "Fix-it" Mann an idea. Maybe there were kids who wanted bikes but couldn't afford them. He began looking all over his hometown of Belmont, North Carolina—scouring flea markets, sales, and thrift stores—buying up any salvageable bicycle parts. With a chain here, a seat there, and a body here, he recycled the cycles into ridable bikes and filled up his two-story backyard warehouse.

Then he opened the doors to the neighborhood kids. They could come in the morning, check out a bike, ride it until sunset, and return it. With anywhere from 250 to 450 cycles to choose from (depending on the state of Mann's inventory), a borrower could have a different bike for every day of the week.

And so Mann the librarian brought miles of smiles to the children of Belmont. The rules in his "library" were few. No cards, no fines, no charges, and an honor system of checking out the merchandise—there was a clock on the wall, a pad, and a pencil to record names and times.

Mann spent long hours—sometimes until two o'clock in the morning—restoring his rotating, circulating collection. When the youngsters visited, he talked to them about safety and road courtesy. He even loaned his wares to fundraisers, such as the local Baptist Church bike-a-thon.

Jethro Mann would agree that this was hard work. It was part of what he termed "his working relationship with the Lord."

—Story suggested by Arnold Percy

# "IT'S YOURS"

It was not easy finding Carl Kearns at work in the town of Windham, Ohio. He was tucked away in a corner of his nephew's tire-repair shop, where amid cats dozing and violins hanging from a line, he sat at his workbench. A retired photographer, Carl spent his time painstakingly repairing and restoring broken violins.

Where did he get the violins? Usually people brought them to him. They had been found in attics or bought at flea markets, and the owners often thought "they've got a priceless Stradivarius"—as Carl said with a smile. Of course, most of the violins were nowhere near that valuable, and when Carl mentioned the cost of reconditioning, the owners decided to sell them for whatever they were worth. And Carl was often willing to pay more than what they were worth, but he had his reasons.

One of those "reasons" came from a time when some of the best young violinists in the world gathered to attend the nearby Cleveland Institute of Music's ENCORE School for Strings, a six-week summer session of intense study and practice. Through a friend, Carl had heard about one young, aspiring virtuoso from a low-income background. The young man could not afford a violin commensurate with his talents. So Carl invited him to his shop and showed him his collection of shiny, restored violins. "Take your pick," Carl said.

The student inspected each instrument carefully, then chose one, tested its strings, placed it under his chin, and began to play. A beautiful, rich vibrato filled the shop. The student smiled.

"It's yours. No charge," Carl said.

At first the musician protested, but when Carl insisted, he accepted and thanked Carl profusely.

"It's my pleasure," Carl said.

This scene was replayed over and over again. "I hate to see a fine old instrument not in use," Carl explained. "It's good to keep them in playing condition. They need to be played—just like people need exercise." And just like eighty-seven-year-old Carl Kearns needed to use his talent for restoring violins.

—H. L. "Bert" Akin

# TOO BUSY TO WORRY

It wasn't unusual to see Eva Miller's old pickup truck parked near the Port Angeles, Washington, dump. For nine years, slender, gray-haired Mrs. Miller had been collecting bicycles, wagon wheels, and other salvageable articles that she repaired for sale in her rummage shop.

Five days a week, from 10:30 in the morning until 4:30 in the afternoon, she was on duty in the shop. When business was slow, she sanded, painted, glued, hammered, or mended toys, carriages, and household articles.

It all started in 1962, when the carefree retirement plans of Ralph Miller, a Washington logger, and his wife, Eva, changed suddenly at the diagnosis of their small grandson's ailment as cystic fibrosis.

When specialists said there was no known cure for cystic fibrosis, but that the victims' suffering could be greatly relieved by therapy and equipment to help breathing, Eva vowed to find some way to help.

Singlehandedly, she earned more than $10,000 for the Seattle Children's Orthopedic Hospital. She did it by running a permanent rummage sale in a cramped, unheated, leaky-roofed building that she rented next door to a tavern. She advertised for castoffs and donations and began the most demanding, yet rewarding, time of her life—aided and encouraged by Mr. Miller.

"Since then I've kept too busy to worry about growing old," she said. "I've always liked restoring things, then finding someone to appreciate and buy them."

She wouldn't mention how much desperately needed equipment had been purchased through her hours of drudgery, preparing material for sale in her rummage shop.

She would simply shrug off praise, saying, "It just takes a lot of faith."

Faith and concern—plus thousands of long, cold hours of fingernail-breaking work among other people's discards.

—Story suggested by Genevieve H. Miller

# "IT'S A GIFT"

Every morning that she could, a petite, white-haired woman clutching a small black purse walked into a courtroom in Los Angeles and found a seat. Grace Robertson, retired at age seventy-eight, was not fascinated by law, nor was she a thrill-seeker.

She knew that every now and then in that courtroom, she would be able to help someone.

The first time was when a distraught woman was about to lose her dog because she didn't have enough money to pay for the license. Mrs. Robertson stepped up and provided the money.

When the tearful dog lover offered to pay her back "soon," Grace Robertson shook her head.

"It's a gift."

For years the white-haired widow helped people that way, with small sums. It was "her gift to God," as she described it. Once she stepped forward to pay the fine of a twenty-one-year-old boy who had no money and was about to be jailed for a minor offense. When the surprised judge asked her why she wanted to pay the $50 fine, Mrs. Robertson replied: "When they take away your freedom, there is so little left. I have saved a few dollars for bus fare to Omaha. My husband and daughter are buried there. But I can wait."

Touched, the judge reduced the fine to five dollars. A newspaper reporter in court wrote the story for a news service. As a result, the troubled boy was reunited with his New England parents, who had not heard from him in two years.

Naturally, Mrs. Robertson was pleased with that happy ending. But she wasn't prepared for the onslaught of mail that came her way.

"I certainly didn't do this for publicity," she said.

Eventually, she realized her dream and was able to visit the graves of her family members in Omaha.

But she didn't stay long. She had to return to a courtroom in Los Angeles, where she was sure somebody would need her again.

—Story suggested by H. M. Ulrich

# HAPPY BIRTHDAY, JESUS!

Because Nicolosa Donlucas had fifty cents, hands for work, and a heart for love, 104 poor Mexicans celebrated Christmas one year.

Nicolosa—a custodian at the Plaza Community Center in Los Angeles, earned $90 a month. She spoke no English, but one summer day the Rev. Nicolas Davila, minister at the Center, told her, in Spanish, the parable of the talents—how from a little, much good could come. And the minister dropped a half dollar into the charlady's hand.

"This is a talent," he said. "Use it wisely, and it will increase."

Nicolosa looked at the coin in her work-gnarled hand and considered the parable. Surely it was more than a story. . . .

Some days later, Nicolosa timidly approached the minister and handed him $17.50.

"This is for the Center," she said. And she explained how she had taken the fifty cents and bought cheese and tortillas. She had then made enchiladas and sold them to neighbors, continuing the operation until she had $35. Half was for the Center,

118

and the other half she would use to make more enchiladas when the cleaning chores were over.

"This is what the story meant, is it not so?" she said before returning to her work.

One day Nicolosa showed the minister a bankbook—she had earned $100 making enchiladas.

The money was not for herself. She knew only too well how many poor people there were in Mexico, and so she had written to her brother there for the names of thirty-three orphans in his village of San Luis, and the names of thirty-three orphans in the town of Nochistalin. She also wrote to another brother in Mexico for the names of thirty-three elderly people who were alone or hungry.

And so, when Christmas morning arrived, sixty-six orphans and thirty-three elderly people received a gift from the custodian. There was even a little money left to brighten the day for four prisoners in Mexican jails.

When Nicolosa told the minister of her plans, he had asked, "But why thirty-three orphans and thirty-three old people?"

"Because that is the number of years Jesus lived," Nicolosa explained. "I want to say 'Happy Birthday to Baby Jesus.'"

And Nicolosa Donlucas did so by using her talent and her heart.

—Richard Mathison

# FOOD FOR ALL

You might have seen them at the checkout counter of your grocery store: bar-coded cards labeled "Food for All." The cards were a convenient way for shoppers to help feed needy persons. You chose how much you would like to donate—from fifty cents to five dollars—and when the clerk rang up the cards along with your groceries, you ended up buying food for hungry people, too.

The cards were the brainstorm of Linda Hamilton, age forty-seven, the mother of two sons and the wife of a Southern California clergyman. Linda had once heard a sermon that dramatized the needs of the poor. "I couldn't believe that fifteen percent of the world's population used eighty-five percent of its resources," she said. Inspired by that message, Linda began working in inner-city churches across the United States, often helping hungry people. Then she came up with the idea for Food for All.

"My husband and I often donated canned goods from the supermarket to various hunger groups," she explained, "but it didn't seem a very efficient way to give food to the needy. It was piecemeal, one can at a time." One evening she was paying her gas bill when she noticed that the utility company had a winter assistance program. "You could add an additional amount to help people who couldn't pay their own bills."

With this idea in mind, Linda came up with her fund-raising method. Her biggest difficulty was in convincing grocery stores that it would work. The first supermarket to try it was an independent store in Redlands; then came the large Lucky Stores chain in California. Soon, Food for All had cards for people to purchase in more than a thousand supermarkets nationwide.

Linda's nonprofit organization collected the funds and made grants to various church soup kitchens, food pantries, and international self-help hunger groups. Ten percent went toward administrative costs, and the rest was distributed. Linda's volunteer work eventually turned into a full-time job for her. She was joined by a paid staff of ten, but they depended on hundreds of volunteers as they dispersed the money here and abroad.

Food for All raised literally millions for worthy groups. What began as Linda's desire to help others ended up bringing the world a little closer to food for all.

# THE PIE MAN

Richard Henry trimmed off the ragged edges of dough hanging over the rim of a pie tin. He swiveled around in his chair at the kitchen table and slid the tin across the green breakfast counter, where thirty other crust-covered, six-inch pie tins were waiting to be filled.

During the day Richard worked in a furniture store in Phoenix, Arizona. But on Tuesday evenings he went home and baked—sometimes until three in the morning—making sixty to a hundred pies a night.

On Wednesdays, while making his deliveries for the store, he sold his pies to customers—upholsterers, drapery suppliers, and the like. Many people paid more than the seventy-five-cent price of each pie because they knew the proceeds went to First Church of God in Christ, where Richard was a Sunday school superintendent and deacon.

His pie-baking talent was a "God-given gift," said Richard, a soft-spoken, sixty-year-old man.

It all began one February, when he had been asked to assist with a special anniversary offering for the pastor.

122

"I didn't want to just ask people to give money, so I asked the Lord to give me something that would help me make money, and this is what he told me to do," Richard said.

He had never baked a pie before that day.

On a typical Wednesday, all the pies had been sold by early afternoon. The money was kept in a special account until Richard made one big contribution. His pie sales brought the church $1,500 to $2,000 each year—over and above Richard's regular weekly offerings. The donations were used to pay for a new organ, remodel the church building, aid needy families, and support other projects.

"I enjoy baking. It gives me a chance to do something for my church that I wouldn't be able to do otherwise," said the Pie Man of Phoenix as he pushed a tray of seventeen lemon meringues into the bottom of his double oven.

—Cheryl Crooks

# CATCH HANDS AND SING

A hospital room in Muskegon, Michigan; a dying man; a motherly woman at his bedside. When she took his hand and began singing softly, "He touched me, he touched me," the dark clouds seemed to lift; the patient's fears faded away.

The singer was Deborah Alexander, wife of Lavern Alexander and mother of seven. She was a medication administration technician in the cancer unit at Hackley Hospital and a locally recognized gospel singer.

Years before, as a nurse's aide, Deobrah had been tending an eighty-six-year-old man bedridden with cancer. "He was so weak that he couldn't say any words," she recalled, "but when I started singing he seemed to perk up. He began singing along with me. From then on we sang together during my shifts, hymns like 'I Must Tell Jesus' and 'His Eye Is on the Sparrow.' When he died three weeks later, his family asked me to sing at his funeral."

That was the beginning of Deborah's musical work.

Word of this volunteer ministry soon got around the hospital. Deborah tried to fill every request for her singing, but after a while, feeling emotionally drained, she took a leave of absence to be a full-time wife and mother.

During her leave, however, Deborah felt God telling her to return to Hackley. "All right, Lord," she said one day, "I'm available to you." So back to the cancer unit she went.

As Deborah went from room to room giving medications, she looked for a sign—a Bible or a religious card or symbol on a patient's bedside table. Sometimes a patient would ask her to pray. "I don't preach," she said. "I just 'catch hands' and sing."

Deborah had no regrets about being a part-time staff worker and a full-time "minister of music." Every two months there was a memorial service at the hospital for those cancer patients who had died. Family and friends of the patients were invited, and Deborah sang. Once, after one of the services, a family member came up and thanked her, saying, "You were an answer to our prayers."

And that was exactly what Deborah Alexander hoped to be.

—Loretta Robinson

# TALENT TO BE TAPPED

The audience in the auditorium grew quiet as fifteen women in pale blue gowns and eight men wearing navy blue suits filed in and took their places on the stage. The lights dimmed. Then an attractive, blond woman positioned herself in front of the singers. Marilyn Mills was about to direct a concert by the Goldenaires—a group whose ages ranged from sixty-five to eighty-five!

Inspiration for starting the group came to Mrs. Mills unexpectedly. A mother of two teenage sons and an active community worker, she found herself with a growing desire to work with elderly people. This led her to sign up for a course in gerontology at a nearby college.

One of her first assignments was to visit several senior centers. Frequently at these places the men and women were gathered around a piano enjoying a "sing-along." Mrs. Mills, a talented musician who had directed many choruses and knew the joy of group singing, could tell that many of the voices she was hearing defied the notion that older people lose their ability to sing well.

"They were God-given talents waiting to be tapped," she said. So she contacted local nursing homes and retirement centers and announced that rehearsals for a seniors choral group would be held at her house every Tuesday morning. She even volunteered to provide transportation in her station wagon! Six prospective singers showed up for that first session.

As the group grew in size, they continued to practice at Marilyn's home for two hours every Tuesday. They sang everything—Gershwin, Cole Porter, and pop and folk music, as well as special holiday numbers. And they never wanted for places to perform. Requests poured in to the Goldenaires from everywhere—hospitals, retirement homes, women's clubs, churches, synagogues, Elks Club, singles groups.

The Goldenaires accepted them all, because they loved to sing, and they loved the spirit of caring that developed among the singers, who were of different backgrounds and faiths.

How do I know all this? Why, I am one of Marilyn Mills' Goldenaires.

—Irene Dodson

# RECYCLED MUSIC

Jazz musician Brad Terry of Bath, Maine, was giving workshops to schoolchildren when he noticed that there were plenty who had the talent and desire to play instruments. What they did not have was an instrument to play, and their families didn't have the money to rent one.

Brad realized that lots of people must have old trumpets, clarinets, and such just lying around gathering dust. And so "Encore" was born—a recycling system whereby Terry received donations of old instruments and recycled them to give to kids who wanted to play.

Such a simple idea that did so much good.

It got me thinking. Attics, basements, cellars, even "junk drawers"—I could almost hear an orchestra (played on recycled instruments, of course) if I set about cleaning them out.

For the very first time, I cleaned my "junk closet" with enthusiasm and a sense of purpose. Those dresses I was saving until I lost ten pounds—off they went to Goodwill. That recorder that I was going to learn to play someday—maybe a budding musician could use it. Those rolls of old linoleum and wallpaper—surely, a kindergarten teacher would love them as art supplies. And all those old eyeglasses could go to New Eyes for the Needy.

Those old possessions weren't junk at all. They were someone else's treasures, just waiting to be sent on to a new life.

—Linda Neukrug

# ACTIVE CONCERN

It looked like a loving family group visiting a relative when Florence and Paul Highfield and their five young children shared a picnic lunch with an inmate behind the gates of an Ohio prison. But the Highfields of rural New Waterford, Ohio, were simply following up a pen-pal project Mrs. Highfield had begun.

"I like people and wanted to help just one other person," she recalled. "The children were too small for me to leave, and praying for unfortunates wasn't enough. Christ meant for us to be active in our concern. That's when I thought of writing letters to friendless prisoners."

The letter writing expanded to include personal visits to the prisoner correspondents from the Highfield family. Paul, a truck driver by trade, transported his wife and family to the prison; the five Highfield children, including twin girls, helped with their friendly, easy acceptance of the men behind bars.

Because of costs and the time involved, Florence couldn't do all the writing and visiting she would have liked. So she worked to involve others in her project.

Upon their release, the inmates she had befriended also helped. There was Tommy, with whom Florence corresponded for five years. Having spent almost half of his thirty-five years behind bars, Tommy was free and in the process of setting up his own sign shop. A frequent visitor in the Highfield home, he had appeared on local TV stations with Florence to enlist others in the pen-pal project because it had helped him so much.

Contact with the outside world was a real help in the rehabilitation of a prisoner. "I try to develop a positive outlook in the inmate, encouraging him to mend family bonds broken by stress and to have faith in God," Florence said.

Florence sent seeds, yarn, fabric, and other items to prisoners for projects the men had started. She also sent them packages when permitted—mainly jelly and homemade goodies from her kitchen. The children helped her, learning firsthand the nature and expression of real concern for others.

A prisoner once wrote to the Highfields, saying, "I am all alone and unloved. I need a friend." The Highfields hoped, with the aid of as many others as they could enlist, to help such men. Florence summed it up by saying, "Every person has the talent to reach out and enlarge the circle of concern."

# HOMEGROWN MINISTRY

Scott Williams, a Pennsylvania attorney, and his wife, Carol, regularly went to prison. No, they weren't convicts behind bars. The Williamsport couple was part of a prison fellowship, and for several years, through their United Methodist church's lay-witness mission, they visited women inmates at Pennsylvania's State Correctional Institution at Muncy.

The Williamses became involved when they were distressed to learn that if a woman was pregnant at the time of her sentencing and had no family to care for her baby after the birth, the child was taken away to a foster home, often many miles away. Sometimes the mother never saw her child again.

Scott contacted the prison's office and let it be known that his legal services were available without charge to any mother wishing to place her child in a temporary home until the time of her release. Then the Williamses set about recruiting Christian families who lived near the prison. They would receive no payment for their parenting, and they had to agree to give up the child when the mother was released.

132

Dr. and Mrs. Gary Berger of Hughesville took a child into their home. The Bergers took the baby boy to see his mother every week and on special holidays. When the mother was released, the Bergers helped her find a job and an apartment.

John and Loretta Shimko of Muncy volunteered to take a prisoner's baby a few months after their own baby had died at birth. "Having this child in our house has helped us get over our loss," they said. "It has blessed our lives."

Another couple, whose own brood of eighteen had left the nest, took in one of the prison babies because they couldn't imagine life without a child in the house.

This homegrown ministry not only gave babies a foster family, but also, through weekly prison visits, made a mother feel that she too was part of a family. And, as Scott Williams pointed out, "It helps the mother know that she has worth in the eyes of God."

—Jane Douglass White

# THE SHUTTLE SERVICE

After their son had been convicted of robbery and sent to prison, Cecelia and James Whitfield of Indianapolis, Indiana, visited him regularly. Each time, they couldn't help noticing the sorrowful looks of prisoners who never seemed to have any visitors. The Whitfields learned that only a small percentage of the inmates received visitors, because their families—many of whom lacked cars and had to depend on public transportation—found it difficult getting to the out-of-the-way prison.

"James," Cecelia said to her husband one day as they drove home, "let's start a shuttle service."

It was probably fortunate that the Whitfields, with their modest incomes (he was a machinist's repairman; she was a computer operator), did not try to figure out whether it could be done; they just did it.

Cecelia contacted a bus company and asked them to put a secondhand vehicle on layaway. James sought financial help from their friends and church, Metropolitan Baptist. They borrowed money from the equity on James's mother's house.

134

Six months later the Whitfields paid $4,000 for a sixty-six-passenger bus. Then they recruited retired bus drivers (headed by Cecelia's uncle) and set up a visitation program.

Two days a week and on Saturdays and Sundays, at a convenient location near the Indianapolis-Marion County Public Library, the bus picked up friends and relatives of the men behind bars. A rotating monthly schedule took the bus to eight different prisons.

But those trips did more than just get people to the prisons. James and Cecelia encouraged their passengers to get to know one another and form support groups. The Whitfields were quick to talk about their own sorrow, and they emphasized that it was their faith in God that sustained them. At the end of the trip each rider received a Precious Bible Promises book.

At the prison, the Whitfields made a point of spending time with the inmates who did not receive visitors. Cecelia and James invited the men to call them collect if they wanted to talk between visits.

Their son was released from prison, but Cecelia and James continued their work. And they turned their own heartache into a blessing for others.

—Patricia Walworth Wood

# STOCKADE ANNIE

Each Sunday the doors swung open from the cell block of the stockade at Fort Campbell, Kentucky, and prisoners filed into the chapel for an hour with eighty-seven-year-old Mrs. Anna Mabry Barr. To thousands of hospitalized or imprisoned soldiers, she was "Stockade Annie."

It was a title compounded of respect and admiration.

More than twenty years before—raw with grief over the death of her minister husband, and with no children—she "argued" with God about being alive. "Why did you leave me behind?" she cried.

The answer came in a crowded bus station on Mother's Day in 1943, when she saw a wounded soldier wearing a white carnation on his uniform. He seemed so forlorn. She thought of other wounded soldiers, still in the military hospital nearby. She hurried to a florist and soon was in a taxi, loaded with flowers, on her way to the hospital. She had been "on duty" ever since, relaying messages to parents and wives, comforting the sick and fearful, and telling the men of the divine help awaiting their calls.

In 1944 she added the stockade to her rounds, though it took a year of perseverance before she received a pass—the only such pass that had ever been given to a civilian.

At her own expense, Mrs. Barr had more than fifty-five thousand copies of Psalm 91 printed in a small white folder, titled, "The Soldier's Psalm." Once when she was handing them out in a bus station, a serviceman pulled out his tattered duplicate and said, "You gave me this in 1943."

Another soldier was one she helped exonerate of an alleged crime. Finally free, he wrote that he was building a chapel in his home community.

"I found him in solitary and always have remembered his first prayer. It was so direct that I often repeat it to those who ask how to contact God," she said.

The soldier had knelt by her on the floor of his cell and opened his heart: "God, if you are there like she says; if you can hear me; if you do hear me; if you can help me; if you will help me; please, help me. And if you let me know what you want me to do so I'll know you want me to do it, I'll try to do it."

Later he confided, "You can't see the wind, but you sure know when it's blowing on you."

Mrs. Barr knew the sensation because she had felt it at the time when, in her own grief, she had been given the answer to, "Why did you leave me here?"

—Herndon Medlock

137

# "I HAD TO DO SOMETHING"

Noreen Lawless, consumer loan manager of the Suburban Bank in Norristown, Pennsylvania, noticed that a customer wasn't keeping up on his loan payments. Being new on the job, she was worried. Perhaps she had approved a loan unwisely. Checking further, she found that a large percentage of other borrowers hadn't made their payments.

The first delinquent customer Noreen telephoned for an explanation was irate. "How can you expect me to pay back a loan when I'm out of work?" the man yelled. Several others she called revealed similar predicaments. Unemployment—due to a slumping economy and the closing down of several key Norristown factories—not sickness or poor budgeting—was causing the alarmingly high number of delinquent payments.

The more Noreen studied the problem, the greater her concern about it became. The gravity of the situation was even more apparent to her when she phoned one man, age forty-three and the father of three children. He had a big mortgage and his wife was threatening to leave him, he said. He had not worked in the past nine months and was talking about suicide.

"I had to do something after that," Noreen says. "The loans were an important part of my life. But it was the people and their problems I really related to."

Unsure about how to proceed, Noreen's answer came when a bank customer, a man who headed an electronics firm, heard of her concern and said he had some jobs available. Noreen began making calls, telling customers she knew where they might find employment. Most of the people she talked to were taken aback. "I've never heard of anybody at a bank trying to find people jobs," one man said.

Working long after her regular hours ended each day, Noreen kept on trying to find jobless people work—any kind of work. A forty-year-old salesman, who was trying to put one child through college and had another at home—along with a sick wife—was glad to repair a friend's garage door. A mechanic, anxious to put a week's groceries on the table, took a small house-painting job that Noreen located for him. An engineer jumped at the chance to do some maintenance work she had heard about.

Thanks to an unusual loan manager, a good many lives in Norristown began to turn around, families were able to stabilize, and customers were coming back to Noreen to thank her. The bank's delinquency rate also decreased, but Noreen found that her real satisfaction came from that extra little step she took. "I'm just thankful I could do anything at all for those people who needed help," she said.

—Toby Smith

# JUSTICE FOR THE POOR

With its shelves of Bibles, concordances, and atlases, the library at Grace United Methodist Church in East Dallas, Texas, didn't look like a courtroom. And the man who sat at one table didn't look like a courtroom judge. He wore no robes, he didn't give instructions to a jury, he didn't even get paid. And yet the decisions Merrill Hartman made on Thursday nights were as binding as any he made during the day in the 192nd Civil District Court.

Judge Merrill Hartman started his unusual night court in a roundabout way. As an attorney with a small practice specializing in trial law, he was representing a client in Puerto Rico. The sight of needy children there pricked his conscience. He thought of children like them he had seen in Dallas. What could he do for them and their parents?

Back home in Dallas, Hartman began visiting a poor section of the city, where he and two other lawyers started a clinic, offering free legal help to the people there. Soon other lawyers joined them, and more legal clinics sprang up.

Then in the mid-1980s, his career took a big change when he ran for judge. Once elected, however, he was not able to volunteer at the legal clinic; judges are not allowed to practice law. How could he continue to serve the poor?

Several months after his election, Hartman was asked by a local reporter how he planned to help the legal clinics. Without having ever thought about it before, he announced, "I'm going to hold court at them."

And so one evening a week, that's what he did, sitting in a church library to hear uncontested family-law matters. Because this court was in session at night, volunteer attorneys were easier to find; these cases didn't take them away from the office during the most productive hours of the day. Similarly, clients usually didn't have to miss work.

Hartman shared his "bench" with three other volunteer judges. It was a unique concept in American jurisprudence, and it all got started because Judge Hartman sought a way to serve God. "The gospel is about justice for the poor," he says, "and this is something God has equipped me to do."

# TREE OF LIFE

It bothered Dušan Bernić to see so many unemployed young people on the streets of New York City with nothing to do, no place to go. So he taught some of them to cook.

Mr. Bernić was owner and chef of the Terrace, a popular and elegant Manhattan restaurant. Dušan worked hard for his success. And he worked hard to help others.

"God and this country have been good to me," he said. "I want to give something back." So he invited poor and disadvantaged young people into the kitchen of the Terrace to learn the details of preparing and serving the finest in haute cuisine.

For years, chef Bernić conducted classes for students who met in small groups several times a week. Boys and girls were referred by community-service agencies, high-school youth boards, and various churches and schools throughout the city. In the buzz of a big-city kitchen, they learned how to chop and carve and blend and roast everything from duck and oysters to pasta-made-from-scratch and raspberry tarts.

They learned about garniture—the art of adding special touches and trimmings to food. And they were taught the importance of sanitary conditions, about details of timing and coordination and serving procedures—everything they would need to know to qualify for restaurant jobs in the outside world. It was training that could cost many thousands of dollars to obtain in cooking and hotel schools in the United States and Europe.

A number of Dušan's students "graduated" to good restaurant jobs of their own, and such positive results prompted him to start a foundation called Tree of Life, which he hoped would help alleviate hunger and poverty here and abroad.

No one knew better than Dušan how cooking skills could translate into personal success and satisfaction. He had attended hotel school in his native Yugoslavia, and after fleeing across the border to Austria and emigrating to the United States, got a job at the New York hotel. He went to school in his off hours to earn a degree in hotel management. Better and better jobs followed—until finally Dušan was the owner of his own fine restaurant.

Dušan's wife, Nada, trained at hotel school also, but spent much of her time teaching handicrafts and sewing to blind and deaf persons in nursing homes and schools. Both Bernićs loved to work with their hands, and in so doing passed along real skills that elevated and enriched others. "I do not wish to accumulate money," Dušan said. "This is my purpose in life."

# KJ'S KIDS

For eight months of the year Kevin Johnson was on the go—dribbling, passing, and shooting the basketball for the Phoenix Suns. In fact, one year, the six-foot, one-inch All-Star guard led his team in scoring, assists, and steals—helping them win a spot in the NBA play-offs. But even when he was on the road, KJ never lost touch with a group of kids back in his hometown neighborhood in Sacramento, California.

They were the children of St. Hope Academy, an after-school and summer program that KJ had started for disadvantaged boys and girls, ages eight to eighteen. Whenever he was off court, he was always writing or calling them, exhorting them to do their best.

The program began when KJ was back home and discovered that he was the only one from his group of childhood friends to leave his tough Oak Park area. Why had he succeeded where others had failed? He knew it wasn't just athletic talent. He had to give credit to the love and support of his mother and grandparents who helped raise him. That encouragement was something he could give to the kids who still lived in Oak Park.

During the year, the program ran with the assistance of paid instructors who helped the youngsters with academics and instilled in them strong moral values. And in the off-season, during the summertime, KJ spent seventy-hour weeks at St. Hope. He talked to the kids, encouraging them to get good grades, stay in school, and go to college. He could point to his own academic and athletic success (when he graduated from the University of California at Berkeley, he was the school's all-time career scorer—1,655 points). And yes, he shot a few baskets with the kids.

Many professional athletes sponsor worthy causes for children, but few have spent as much time as KJ working with the kids themselves. He knew the St. Hope kids by name and could identify their strengths and weaknesses. "They see that I've come from the same place," he said, "and that they can have a sense of pride and dignity in who they are and where they're from."

KJ cited his own rewards for his work at St. Hope's. "The Bible teaches that children are a heritage from the Lord. So if I'm doing something to nurture that heritage, then I'm doing my job for the Lord. And if I put a smile on a kid's face, that's enough for me."

—Gina Bridgeman

# MORE THAN A NAME

The chef was French; the kitchen was in the Beth Abraham Nursing Home in New York's Bronx. Gerard Potel, age forty-four and once the personal chef to French President Georges Pompidou, prepared food for fragile and elderly diners, most of whom were on Medicaid.

As a young man Gerard had started medical school, but at age twenty he turned to the culinary trade, following in his father's (and his father's father's) footsteps. For generations the Potels have satisfied discriminating palates at their restaurant in Paris. Then Gerard made what was supposed to be a brief visit to the United States.

During his stay Gerard heard that Beth Abraham was looking for a chef, and on a whim he visited the nursing home. After inspecting the kitchen, he took a walk through the halls and talked with some of the residents. "I fell in love with them," he said. Gerard returned to Paris just long enough to pack his bags.

The challenges at the nursing home proved monumental. He and his staff prepared two thousand meals a day—the majority of them for seniors with restricted diets. That meant hundreds of specialized meals every day. Gerard encouraged his staff to get out of the kitchen and visit the residents to learn their likes and dislikes. He wanted the patients to be considered more than just names on trays.

Often he worked with those on feeding tubes. Together with the medical staff, he tried to find favorite foods that those patients could manage to chew and swallow. He was especially pleased when someone was able to go from pureed to solid food. And unlike most chefs, Gerard delighted in complaints. "When someone tells me a recipe was better two months ago when I used tarragon instead of basil, I'm very happy. It shows that a patient is responding to life."

Nursing home mealtimes are often highlights in a patient's day. At Beth Abraham, patients could look forward to something special from this medical-student-turned-chef, who combined his passions for healing the sick and satisfying the taste buds.

"It's my harbor," Gerard said. "It's where I can do something good for God."

—Pat Brewster

# LEAVE THE DOOR OPEN

For fifty years Bob Garland weathered rain, sleet, and snow to deliver milk to people in the north-central Maine town of Anson. Yet if you had asked an Anson native, "What does Bob Garland do?" you would most likely hear some answers that didn't mention milk at all.

"Once, he fixed my sump pump," said an elderly woman. "He also feeds my cats when I'm away."

"He gave me a jump when my car wouldn't start," said a father of three. "And one time, my wife accidentally left the stove on when we went out. Thank God, Bob came by and smelled something burning."

Bob Garland, Anson's sixty-nine-year-old milkman, was also known to change lightbulbs, pick up extra groceries, shovel sidewalks, and sometimes just sit and talk with customers. "It only takes a few extra minutes," he said. "And I enjoy it."

But those minutes added up. Bob logged six hundred miles a week serving the needs of some two hundred and fifty customers. And though he had help from two employees, including his grandson, Robbie, Bob did most of the work himself—seven days a week, sometimes fourteen or fifteen hours a day. With his busy schedule, his wife, Virginia, admitted with a smile, "If he didn't come home for a bite to eat around ten at night, I might not see him at all."

Besides being Anson's milkman, Bob also served as a city selectman for years. Because of his civic duties, his milk deliveries often didn't start until evening—and didn't finish until late at night. A problem? Hardly. "My customers just go to sleep and leave the door open," Bob said. "I go in, put the milk in the fridge, and lock up."

He was proud to say that his tiny company had "never not operated a day, even if it meant working clear through till morning." And if you mentioned retirement, he responded, "The satisfaction of doing some good for somebody keeps me going. . . . Part of my faith is helping others."

He did get recognition for his loyal service. Once a talk show offered to fly him to Hollywood to appear on network TV. Bob didn't hesitate to answer. "I couldn't," he explained. "Who'd deliver the milk?"

# THE SAME SIDE OF THE TABLE

It was late at night in a Sunday school classroom in Southern California. Harsh words were being exchanged between two brothers who had once been business partners. Caught in the crossfire was Randy Lowry, a volunteer with the Christian Conciliation Service who had been called in to mediate the dispute.

For Randy this was a real busman's holiday. He was an attorney and a professor at Pepperdine University School of Law in Malibu, California, and the director of the school's Institute for Dispute Resolution. He trained students as mediators and consulted with large firms on conflict management. But his work with the Christian Coalition Service was different.

"As a lawyer," he said, "I'm trying to resolve conflicts in ways that are more efficient and more respectful of people than litigation. CCS is an important dimension of that. It combines my legal skills with my personal convictions."

Randy believed that there was a better way to deal with conflict than going to court. He cited the Bible, especially Matthew 18:15-17, in which Christ tells us that if we can't settle a dispute privately, or with just a few witnesses, we should take it to the church. "CCS," he said, "gives me a chance to do that."

As a mediator, Randy worked with families that were splitting up, business partners who were on the verge of suing each other, or churches arguing over property or programs. "Usually by the time I come in, the conflict is acute."

Randy tried to get opposing sides to voice their concerns and focus on the substance of the problems, not the people involved. Then he helped them look for creative solutions. "I want them to get from being on two sides of the table arguing, to being on the same side of the table looking at the problem being solved."

The father of three children, Randy was a busy man. He coached his daughter's soccer team and his son's Little League team. He taught Sunday school at Conejo Valley Church of Christ, and directed music during services. But he found some of the greatest satisfaction in helping people resolve their conflicts.

"It's exciting to see people work through a problem and come to have a relationship in Christ," he said.

*"First be reconciled to your brother, and then come and offer your gift,"* Christ said. Reconciliation—that's Randy's work.

—Kenneth Meeks

# "HELP YOURSELF"

The long-haired teenager knocked on the door of the modest home in Antioch, California. "Someone told me that I could get some free clothes here," he explained hesitantly to the pleasant woman who answered.

The woman invited him in and showed him to a room filled with stacks and racks of clothing. "Help yourself to whatever you can use," she said. As the young man found a pair of slacks, some shoes, and a shirt that fit, he told her how he had hitchhiked from the South without any baggage, but now desperately needed an outfit that would be right for a job interview. Someone had sent him to her house.

Kay DeHart nodded. It often happened like that. Strangers frequently found their way to her "Community Closet," sometimes late at night.

The DeHart "Community Closet" was actually a spare bedroom full of clothing, small household items, linens, and dishes that had come mostly through Kay's church and from the public school's lost-and-found. Women of her Covenant congregation often helped with the washing, mending, and ironing

152

so that the clothes would be ready when needed. Sometimes, if there seemed to be an excess, Kay sent packages to an orphanage in Mexico, a mission in Texas, or the victims of an earthquake or flood.

The Closet began when Kay's fifty-nine-year-old husband, Rex, had a remission from cancer. It was their way of saying "Thank You" to God. After Rex died, Kay went on with the work. And there were hundreds of people who were grateful that she did—people like the seventy-year-old man who found a crutch that he couldn't afford to buy, and a young Vietnamese family who had come as penniless war refugees. They found school clothes for their four children.

Kay DeHart enjoyed what she did, and even though she lived on a very limited income and suffered from a heart condition, she was determined to continue.

"As a child we were very poor, and I used to dream of a day when I would be rich and could help others," Kay mused. "But God has shown me that you don't have to be rich, just give what you have. After all, the Bible tells us that whatever we do to others, we do to the Lord."

—Mary Kentra Ericsson

# ON THE GIVING END

No car had seen the inside of Marguerite Rowlee's Lincoln, Nebraska, garage for years. That was because the space was filled to overflowing with clothing, bedding, furniture—items that Mrs. Rowlee gave away to needy people.

At ninety-two, Mrs. Rowlee had been on the giving end almost all of her life. The youngest of nine, raised on a farm in Ithaca, New York, "Peggy" often joined her family in their orchard to pick fruit for people who didn't have any. "We gave away clothes, too," she recalled. "Since my mother was always sewing for us, she'd run up extras for needy neighbors."

During World War I, Peggy worked as a Red Cross nurse and for New York City Welfare. Then she hurried west to marry Howard Rowlee, her college sweetheart, when he won a job as a civil engineer for the Nebraska Highway Department. She and Howard, who died in 1979, had a daughter and a son, and while the children were still young, Peggy had a difficult battle with polio and again later with cancer. Neither one stopped her.

Over the years there was no mystery in the fact that the generous and the needy found their way to her garage. "I trust

154

the Lord to send me both," she said, "and he does." He sent mothers like Charlotte Hoke, who periodically brought her children's outgrown clothing to Peggy. Or like out-of-towners Marge and Alvin Bohling, who once a year drove sixty-five miles from Johnson, Nebraska, in a van filled with quilts and clothes donated by their town's Martin Luther Church.

Everything that arrived was examined and sorted. Often the garage was filled and emptied two or three times a day.

One night Peggy's doorbell rang. At the door was a tall, white-haired man. "I got no money for a birthday present for one of my young'uns," he said.

"What would the child like?" Peggy asked.

"A piggy bank," he replied.

She went off, then returned with a bright red piggy bank and toys for his twelve other grandchildren. "The night before, a man I'd never seen drove up with a truckload of toys," Peggy said. "That's not coincidence. The Lord's hand was in it."

The Lord's hand was what Peggy firmly held on to. Though frail, hard-of-hearing, and suffering from cataracts, she still helped her sixty-two-year-old son, Howard Jr.—who lived with her—in his struggle with cerebral palsy. Every Sunday she worshiped at Holy Trinity Episcopal Church, and every Thursday she attended an interfaith prayer group. And in between, the indomitable woman went on giving.

—Rhonda Stransberry

155

# RE-BICYCLING

"Are you the guy who has the free bikes?" asked a young boy as he peered into the vacant store where Henry Perry kept bikes in Oakland, California.

"Sure thing. Take your pick," the bearded, middle-aged postal carrier told the boy, gesturing toward the rows of bikes crowded into the small storefront.

For six years Henry had been lending bicycles to youngsters too poor to own one.

"It started when a neighborhood boy stole my bike. The kid only wanted a ride," Henry recalled. "Lots of kids living in the housing projects are so far down at the bottom of the ladder, they don't think it's wrong to take a bike."

Henry, the father of three grown children, told the boy to come borrow his bike when he wanted a ride. Then he began to collect used bikes. Word spread quickly, and soon as many as thirty or forty kids were lined up, waiting their turn at riding the bikes. In the years that followed, other postal workers helped find more bikes, while the city of Oakland turned over about thirty-five unclaimed ones. Henry

156

himself bought parts to rebuild others, aided by his wife, Althea.

Then a businessman donated the unoccupied storefront to shelter the bikes. Henry had three bicycle drill teams in training, and hoped to find funds to buy uniforms for all the kids.

Many of the youngsters resisted discipline, but Henry found they would listen when something they enjoyed was involved. He hoped to get one message across: "Stand tall. Be proud." Riding a bike, caring for it, and following the rules of safe riding, Henry said, are roads that lead to self-respect.

Once Henry and a group of youngsters were riding their bikes near a church when a woman asked him what he was doing.

"Missionary work," he answered. "I'm looking for lost sheep."

Later he explained, "Jesus told us to help our brother. These small human beings didn't know where they're going. I'm trying to give them some direction."

—Story suggested by Linda Ervin

# GOD'S LIST

Shirley Wilson of Great Falls, Montana, loved baby showers, especially when they were for her. The mother of three daughters—two grown and one a teenager—loved showers because they replenished her supply of items for other mothers with newborn babies.

Years earlier Shirley had heard about a new mother who couldn't afford to buy clothing and necessities for her newborn. Shirley had some still-usable garments that her own girls had outgrown, so she took those over to the hospital. And she continued making visits like that.

With help from friends and fellow parishioners of St. Luke's Catholic Church, Shirley collected all sorts of items that a new mother might need. Everything was stored in the basement of her home. When she learned—usually through her church or the welfare department—of a new mother whose husband was unemployed or an unwed mother with no family to help her, Shirley set off on her rounds.

"Having both new and used items is wonderful," Shirley said, "because I'm able to give the mothers at least one thing that is brand-new." Often Shirley lingered to teach a new mother how to care for her baby, or even how to cook.

One afternoon Shirley visited a family and found three children who needed new boots in size one or two. "Let's just put this on God's list," she told the parents.

Shirley had barely arrived home when a neighbor across the street, the mother of triplets, phoned to ask if anyone could use three pairs of boots, all size two. "It was just like the biblical story of the loaves and the fishes," Shirley marveled.

Shirley Wilson's generosity was instilled in her by her mother who, although she had eleven children of her own, always gave food and clothing to those who were less fortunate. "I remember thinking," Shirley said, "I'm going to do that when I grow up."

—Roberta Donovan

# GIVE US KNOWLEDGE

Your hands are made for hard work," Harriet Van Meter was told as a child. So, after raising a family, she went back to college and earned two degrees. And she reached out her hands to the first foreign students to arrive at the University of Kentucky.

"No one looked after them," she said. "So I did." For ten years she held a Sunday-night open house to bring foreign students together with her American friends. She also started a library in the poorest section of Lexington.

In the 1960s Harriet traveled to India. It was a time of famine and drought, and when Harriet saw the many students lined up outside libraries waiting for their turns to study, she was determined to help. When she returned to Kentucky, Harriet wrote a letter to an Indian newspaper and offered to send books, seeds, or food to anyone there who was interested. After the letter was published, Harriet received four hundred replies! And ninety percent of the letters asked for books.

"If you will give us knowledge," the people said, "we'll take care of the rest."

Harriet telephoned everyone she knew to send her whatever books they could. Working out of her kitchen and basement, and using her own money, she began to mail books abroad. Several of her friends also became excited about the project and asked for names and addresses so that they, too, could send books and pay the mailing costs themselves.

That was the beginning of the International Book Project, Inc., an organization that matched requests from persons around the world with individuals in the United States who had the books, technical journals, and magazines needed. More than a thousand volunteers regularly sent books to families, schools, hospitals, and libraries in developing countries. As books and correspondence were exchanged, many friendships began. Again and again, the letters would end with the words "God bless you."

To keep costs to a minimum, the Project's office was in Harriet's home. Requests for books arrived daily, but one kind outnumbered all the rest: All around the world, people hungered for the Bible. Eventually, Harriet had ten thousand unfilled requests for Bibles; she needed people and money to fill them. But she was confident that the Lord would provide.

"I'm truly convinced that God has led me in this project," she said.

—Patricia Howe

# EXPERT VOLUNTEERS

Henry and Margaret Schaeffer of Sibley, Illinois, always had a passion for hitching a trailer to their pickup and journeying far and wide across America. Often, other couples joined them. Finally, after thirty years of managing a supermarket and a restaurant, the time came for them to retire. More time to see the sights.

But on one trip, they didn't like what they saw at all. "We visited the Red Bird Mission, a Methodist mission to mountain people in Beverly, Kentucky, where my brother is a doctor," Henry said. "Many of its buildings were in need of repair, but there was no money for it. How great it would be, I thought, to get some people together and do the job."

Which gave Henry an idea. Why not form a group of other retired people who liked to travel, and organize them into an experienced labor pool of carpenters, nurses, electricians, and typists? Surely there had to be more worthwhile organizations like Red Bird that could use a gang of expert volunteers.

Indeed there were, and so the Roving Volunteers in Christ's Service—RVICS, for short—was born. The plan was simple: As coordinator, Henry would offer the services of his group in return for a spot to park their trailers.

Since that time, RVICS has completed more than twenty projects in thirteen states, 32,000 hours' worth—a dining room for a missionary training center in Texas, shelving and draperies for Bible colleges in Maryland and Florida, even the construction of a bridge over a small river to help make a northern California church camp accessible.

Bible study groups, hymn-sings, and other nonwork activities fostered a spirit of camaraderie among the volunteers. "We're like one big happy family," Margaret said.

What started as Henry's dream blossomed into four RVICS groups, each one taking an assortment of jobs. Said Henry with a smile, "I guess the good Lord just needed me to get the whole thing organized."

—Deborah Miller

# A Feeling of Accomplishment

When Harry Hale retired as an electrical engineer from the Seattle City Light Company, he immersed himself in his beloved hobbies of fishing and golf. "Six months later," he said, a wry smile crossing his lips, "I was bored to death! I'd take long, aimless walks around Lake Union, trying to shake myself out of my depression. I felt useless."

One of these walks took him by a house that had been home to his closest boyhood friend. "It held so many memories for me, I couldn't resist knocking on its front door."

What he found was a pleasant woman who, with her husband, had established the house as the Open Door Clinic to help young people in trouble. As tactfully as he could, Harry pointed out a broken window in the back door. The woman explained that the Open Door Clinic depended on donations and that it was behind on expenses.

Within an hour Harry had fixed the door. The next day he returned to unclog a drain and set right some electrical problems. "That evening," he said, "I went to bed with a feeling of accomplishment for the first time in nearly a year. Then, at three o'clock in the morning, I suddenly jolted wide awake. I had all the right skills to put the Open Door Clinic in top shape. Right then and there I appointed myself its superintendent of maintenance."

After a few months, when he had the Open Door Clinic fixed up, Harry began to help "fix up" some of the young people who came in for help.

He had particular success in rebuilding relationships between parents and troubled children. He explained it this way: "At first, parents of troubled kids are amazed that a gray-headed old bat like me can identify with their children's problems. But I use my age to soften these parents up. First I tell them that I can remember very well doing some things that could have got me into the same predicaments their kids are in. Then I ask them, if I can remember, why can't they? As soon as parents realize they might have made the same mistakes as their kids, they're on their way to loving them again."

When the Open Door Clinic moved to larger quarters, Harry put in twelve-hour days. "And I loved every minute of it," he said. "Helping others is a two-way street, and it has given me the best years of my life. I guess you could say I'm very lucky."

And so were the troubled kids in Seattle who came to Harry Hale with problems that nobody else seemed to understand.

—Richard Bayne

# THE FLOWER PEOPLE

In 1972, at the age of fifty-five, Overton Crawford was forced for medical reasons to retire from his job as manager of an office furniture and supply business in Austin, Texas. "It was a depressing time for me," he recalled. "I felt useless. I prayed and asked the Lord what I should do."

That same year, Overton and his wife, Maurine, purchased an old house in the tiny mountain town of Ouray, Colorado, nestled amid the high peaks of the San Juan mountains on the western slope of the Rockies. Because the late-1800s house needed fixing up, Overton went to work with hammer and paintbrush. When the house was in order, Overton, who grew up on a farm, turned his thoughts to the garden.

First he set out blue spruce trees. Then he planted scarlet and white petunias, columbine, lupine, Shasta daisies, hollyhocks, and more than seven hundred tulip bulbs. The rear portion of his lot was reserved for roses.

Overton's garden flourished, and soon became a local point of interest. Tourists from two large motels nearby often strolled past the Crawford house to admire the flowers and take pictures. Usually working in the yard when out-of-towners came by, Overton found himself engaged in conversations about seed selections, soil cultivation, and proper watering. He also started giving away rootings and bulbs. "I love it," he said, "when these folks write from all over the country to tell me how well the plants I gave them are doing." Sometimes they just address their letters to "The Flower People, Ouray, Colorado."

In addition to vacationers, senior citizens and patients from a nearby nursing home are bused over to the Crawford place. Once, a busload of seniors eagerly accepted Overton's offer of free iris plants to take back to San Antonio, Texas.

Each Sunday, Overton and Maurine picked large bouquets to adorn the sanctuary of their church, First Southern Baptist. And if any other congregations in the area wanted Overton's flowers, all they had to do was ask. After church, the colorful blooms were taken to the sick and the homebound.

So what Overton Crawford started out to do for himself became a blessing to many. "God has been good to me," he said. "He restored my body and soul through the beauty of his flowers and the joy of giving them to others."

# THE SHAVING MASTER

Every evening between 6:00 and 7:00 P.M. the manager of a feed mill in Edgerton, Wisconsin, packed a little bag and walked rapidly to the nearby local hospital. Inside, he strolled down the hall, poking his head into the room of the first male patient.

"Would you like a shave tonight?" he asked.

There was always a surprised look and usually a bumper crop of whiskers. The visitor then opened his bag, removed an electric shaver, and, chatting cheerily, set to work. A few minutes later he was finished and continuing on his way to the next room, gone almost before the patient could even thank him.

This forty-seven-year-old volunteer barber was Norman Amundson, and over the years he appeared regularly, night after night, and shaved more than thirty thousand patients. It all started when his father-in-law, a patient at the hospital, asked Norman to come and shave him. Norman brought his old-style straight razor, soap, and brush. He did it so efficiently that the roommate of his father-in-law asked for a shave too. And so it began. News of the "shaving master" spread through the entire hospital. Norman responded to the need. Soon he had changed to an electric shaver.

What did hospital authorities think? With orderlies and nurses in short supply, they welcomed it. Said one surgeon, "A clean shave raises a patient's morale." And to Norman Amundson, this giving of self brought a deep and joyous personal satisfaction.

Norman was also active in the community and at a local Lutheran church. Married and the father of two sons, he was an alderman and a member of the volunteer fire department.

A local minister, who once benefited from Norman's free shave, stated, "Shaving a man seems like a simple act, yet it is Christianity at work—a man doing something to show his love for his brother."

—Story suggested by W. D. Chesney

# IN THE MANNER OF THE LORD

In a bleak ward in Chicago's Cook County Hospital, the face of a long-term patient brightened as a petite woman appeared with a brown case in hand. "How is everybody today?" she asked brightly.

Roberta Lilly, age seventy-five, her kindly face beaming, walked from bed to bed, humming a song and spreading cheer. She worked without pay in Cook County Hospital for many years. She washed and cared for the feet of thousands of patients; she fed helpless ones, combed hair, ran errands, and rolled patients in wheelchairs. From her brown case she distributed needed items—combs, razor blades, toothbrushes, bobby pins, pencils. She gave comfort from the Bible and prayed with patients.

Foot care probably best typifies Mrs. Lilly's willingness to serve in the manner of the Lord. The Lord washed the feet of his disciples; Mrs. Lilly massaged patients' feet with ointment that she provided. She said she wouldn't be able to do the strength-taxing job except that God had strengthened her hands for "this good work" (Nehemiah 2:18 KJV).

Mrs. Lilly inherited her job from her husband, Raymond, a former carnival laborer who helped patients at the hospital for almost thirty years. He was the hospital's first black chaplain.

When Raymond died, Roberta talked to God about taking his place. Because of bad health, she was worried about her ability to do it. She decided to make a pact: "Lord, I can't do this work myself; you do it through me. Give me the strength I need and I'll serve you at the hospital."

Just two days after Raymond's funeral, the frail figure of his widow emerged from the early morning darkness into the hospital lobby. She had come to do what she could.

For more than ten years past the usual retirement age, Mrs. Lilly continued her work. She resided in the senior center near the hospital and lived frugally on gifts from a few supporters and on her Social Security pension.

Those who helped Roberta Lilly pointed out that she helped bring God's light into their lives, as well as the lives of her patients.

—James R. Adair

# CRADLED IN GOD'S LOVE

**I**an McCart was an assistant vice president in the New York branch of AMRO, an international bank. But every Thursday night you could find him spending an hour with each of four AIDS patients in St. Luke's-Roosevelt Hospital Center.

McCart remembered well his first visit to a patient, Chris. Conversation was difficult for both until McCart got Chris talking about playing sandlot baseball and fixing motors. One night Chris said, "I never asked, what do you do?"

"Work in a bank," McCart replied, and then he impulsively began talking about his own spiritual journey. "So we're both on the same track," the patient said.

McCart recalled how, at the age of twelve, he had given up going to church. He described the emptiness that had troubled him until years later, when he found himself in church again, this time praying ardently for direction. Then, passing the church bulletin board, he focused on one notice: "Volunteers urgently needed at St. Luke's-Roosevelt Hospital."

McCart was there the next evening in a group that included a lawyer, a housewife, an opera singer, a member of the United

Nations Children's Fund, an advertising executive, a grandmother, and a theology undergraduate. All were volunteers receiving orientation on how to work with AIDS patients. McCart signed up—and met Chris.

When in time Chris died, the nurse asked McCart for help. He washed Chris, wrapped him in the required plastic bag, and gently lifted him onto a gurney. He did the same for two others who died.

But if the hospital was a place of death, McCart also found new life there. One evening, the director of volunteers led him to the pediatrics ward, where six "boarder babies" were sleeping. These little ones, she explained, had been abandoned or had come from drug-addicted mothers, or both, and often waited months for adoption or foster care. What they needed most was to be held and loved. Could he help?

From then on, when McCart left the AIDS ward at 10:00 P.M., he hurried to pediatrics. And when he cradled one of those babies in his arms, the emptiness he once felt was gone; he himself felt cradled in God's love.

—Sidney Fields

# JIMMY BOY

The shiny green and white pickup truck with "Jimmy Boy" painted on it pulled up in front of a modest home in the area around Raleigh, North Carolina, and out jumped Fannie Brown, a lively, gray-haired woman who, with the help of a young man, unloaded a hospital bed and gently maneuvered it through the front door of the house. The young man's wife could now recuperate from her recent operation in her own home.

Seventy-seven-year-old Mrs. Brown, affectionately known as Aunt Fannie, distributed hospital beds, wheelchairs, walkers, and other sickroom equipment and supplies for more than twenty years. She began her lending service when a friend with cancer needed a hospital bed. After locating and borrowing a spare one from the Wake County Health Building, she was told to keep it. After that she accumulated some forty-five beds and a variety of other aids.

Fannie drove more than 300,000 miles in every kind of weather, after she learned to drive at the age of fifty-three. One of her trucks had over 120,000 miles on it when she traded it in; then she bought "Jimmy Boy." Fannie says she "bought it on the excitement plan. I sell preserves and then I can make my monthly payments."

To help finance her service to people who are sick or disabled, Fannie looked after the elderly at the Westhaven Rest Home and sold eggs and chickens. A member of the Church of the Nazarene, she had great confidence in prayer. If something she needed was not available, she said, "I just pray to the Lord and he finds me one from somewhere."

Fannie and her husband, Norman, lived a half mile from where she was born on Route 10, officially named Fannie Brown Road. They had four children, ten grandchildren, and four great-grandchildren.

A special week was proclaimed by the governor to honor Fannie in 1972. Fannie took such fame calmly. "I been doing for folks most of my life," she said in her lyrical country accent. "Wherever there is need, I try to help out."

—Lois Morgan Overby

# ANGELS REALLY FLY

As a former cancer patient, Priscilla Blum knew firsthand how expensive treatment was—and also that patients must sometimes travel long distances to get to one of the nation's twenty-seven comprehensive cancer treatment centers.

Priscilla was a licensed pilot who spent a lot of time at the Westchester County Airport in New York. It was there, one day in 1981, that an idea came to her. She had noticed that some of the numerous corporation-owned planes that flew in and out would at times have empty seats. Why not see if these corporations would fly cancer patients to their medical treatments free, whenever their planes made routine business flights?

Priscilla contacted a friend and recovered cancer patient, Jay Weinberg. Jay was doing volunteer work at the Memorial Sloan-Kettering Cancer Center in New York. After Priscilla told him about her vision, Corporate Angel Network (CAN) was born.

CAN's first passenger was eighteen-year-old Michael Burnett. Michael had just had his leg amputated at Sloan-

Kettering. Christmas was coming. Michael needed additional treatment in New York, and his parents simply could not afford to bring him home to Detroit for the holiday. Priscilla and Jay contacted a company whose plane was scheduled to fly to Detroit on December 22. The Safe Flight Instrument Corporation agreed to take Michael along.

Getting CAN in full operation was not easy. Corporate flight schedules were unpredictable, and cancellations numerous. Yet one such last-minute cancellation provided a big breakthrough. In January 1983, after a Norton Simon flight was canceled, the company's chairman, David Mahoney, telephoned Jay Weinberg to apologize and ask what he could do to help. "Write a letter to your peers telling them about us," Jay answered, "and get it published in a widely read business magazine." The chairman did. As a result, a hundred firms signed up.

CAN has flown thousands of flights, logging more than three million air miles and using over four hundred participating corporations. CAN worked with a small staff of volunteers and a budget of about $100,000, spent mostly on telephone, postage, and two paid employees. There was no active fundraising.

Meanwhile, Priscilla and Jay went right on proving that angels really do fly.

# MORE THAN A NURSE'S AIDE

I had slipped into my nightdress after a shower and wearily sat on the edge of my hospital bed, just as the nurse's aide, Marie Perez, came into the room. She picked up a towel and patted it on my damp hair. Her movements were soothing, tender. The next morning she brought me a square of plastic and a safety pin. She had noticed that I had no shower cap and, unasked, had ingeniously taken care of this slight emergency—thus adding to the comfort of a sick person. She continued such kindnesses daily.

Once I glanced out of my open door and saw Marie scurrying down the corridor. She almost seemed to dance in the sheer ecstasy of performing her duty!

I was deeply impressed with this middle-aged Mexican woman and, inquiring about her, I learned:

Born in Monterey, Mexico, Marie became motherless shortly after birth and fatherless two years later. Her grandparents, both doctors, took over her care. At age nine she was completely orphaned again. Friends of her grandparents took her to San Antonio, Texas, but instead of giving her loving care, they used her as an unpaid household slave. After two years of neglect and unhappiness, Marie became ill.

She was rushed to Santa Rosa Hospital, where she was nursed back to health and nourished with love by the sisters who permitted Marie to remain there.

For more than thirty years Marie had served the hospital, the sisters, and her beloved patients—sewing, upholstering, purchasing supplies, and providing bedside care. When she was thirty-seven years old, Marie earned the title of Nurse's Aide, and after that she devoted all her time to the sick.

She also cared for an incurably sick sister, helped support two nieces, and assumed responsibility for a grandnephew whom she called "Son."

Marie never married—the hospital was her home. In all her years of service, she was absent only twice. And she was on duty at least an hour early every day to make sure that the patients were properly prepared for Holy Communion.

In seeing her devotion to duty, I was reminded of the Bible verse: "Render service with enthusiasm, as to the Lord . . . knowing that whatever good we do, we will receive the same again from the Lord" (Ephesians 6:7-8 NRSV).

—Ida M. Barkan

# A FOOT IN HEAVEN

When Boston bus driver Paul J. Murphy visited a friend, Eleanor Marvin, in Holy Ghost Hospital one day, he became concerned about the multiple sclerosis victim. She had been bedridden for nine years, and her world was small: four walls, a ceiling, and the tiny patch of sky visible from her window.

Paul wondered how he could enlarge her world.

"If an ambulance can bring the sick to the hospital, it can bring them out," the bus driver reasoned.

Paul, who—together with his wife, Helen, and their sixteen-year-old daughter, Mary Elizabeth—lived in Mattapan, Massachusetts, hired an ambulance and two attendants to give Eleanor a three-hour tour of Boston. Fellow bus drivers at Metropolitan Transit Authority contributed $54.10 to help pay the costs. Enough was left over for a special treat.

Freed from the confines of her hospital room, Eleanor enjoyed the drive to historic and scenic places of interest. With her "special treat" money she bought something that she had wanted for a long time—a grilled frankfurter, picnic-style, with all the fixings.

Everything was new and exciting. Jets, to Eleanor, had only been a terrifying noise over the hospital. Seeing one close-up on the airport grounds, she was reassured.

The outing provided dreams and fond memories for days.

After that, Paul spent his free time giving outings to more than 175 people. Then he founded the nonprofit Para Tours to provide free ambulance trips and a "treat on the road" for homebound people unable to go out in a car.

Some had special requests: Nancy Bowser, age twenty-two and paralyzed since birth, had been longing to visit a religious shrine at Ipswich. Her pastor relayed her desire to Paul, and through Para Tours, Nancy spent a wonderful day at the shrine.

These "busman's holidays" continued because of something the very first tour guest had written after her ambulance ride.

"As I rode over the Mystic River Bridge, I looked down on the water and then up to the blue sky," Eleanor Marvin confided. "Suddenly I saw 'The Eyes of God smile down on me,' and on all those wonderful people who had helped to put my foot in heaven."

It was Paul Murphy's fondest hope that the sight-seeing ambulance project might spread to other communities, so that more of the confined would be able "to put a foot in heaven" for a few hours.

—Story suggested by Mrs. William O. Gile

# EVERY CHILD DESERVES A CAKE

When Marian Beach celebrated her seventy-second birthday, her husband, Leonard, gave her a card picturing a woman decorating a cake. Inside it read, "You deserve a cake today. Or two or three or four."

How about 850 cakes? If Marian were to receive a cake for every cake she had baked for someone else, she would deserve every one of them—and more. Marian created, decorated, sculpted, and iced hundreds of cakes for children's birthday parties at the Colorado Christian Home in Denver. The home housed nearly a hundred youngsters from ages five to twelve who suffered from severe emotional problems, so Marian was kept busy all year.

At the beginning of each month, the home sent her a list of upcoming birthdays. Then she went into action. No two children are alike and no two of Marian's cakes were ever the same. She might pour the batter into a plain rectangular pan and then freeze it; and when it was frozen, she would carve out a dog, a cat, a duck, or a tiger. After the cake was baked, she would paint it with frosting—in every color of the rainbow.

Often she looked to the calendar for inspiration. For a July birthday she might make an American flag; for back-to-school birthdays in September, it might be a red apple for the teacher or a lemon-yellow bus. Once, a child couldn't decide between a cake shaped like a skateboard or one depicting Snoopy's crony, Woodstock. She compromised and put Woodstock on a skateboard!

Usually, though, she didn't take orders. She preferred to keep a low profile at Colorado Christian Home. The residents knew her only as "The Birthday Cake Lady," but for those children, often victims of abuse and neglect, her culinary art had an effect all its own.

"Marian's efforts make the children feel special," said David Holmes, director of development at the home. "It's important for our children, who haven't felt that." That was her recipe: Every child is unique in God's sight; every child deserves a cake of his or her very own.

Marian's labor was entirely voluntary, and she paid for her own supplies. She didn't see any prospect of cutting back. She said, "A friend asked me once, 'When are you ever going to stop baking cakes for the children?' I told her, 'Not until my hand shakes and I can't draw a straight line anymore.' "

—Dennis Manoloff

# THE SEWING ANGEL

The little girl posing for her picture was all smiles as she proudly showed off her new dress—the first new dress she had ever received in all her eight years. No wonder she called Velma Fisher "The Sewing Angel."

White-haired Mrs. Fisher, called Tillie by her friends, had been sewing little girls' dresses since she retired at age fifty-five on medical disability due to a hip operation. Before that she had worked for the government for more than thirty years, sewing parachutes. To help pass the time after she retired, she started to sew dresses for a neighbor's three small daughters.

Then, having extra material on hand, she made a few more dresses, but she wondered what she could do with them. She contacted the Salvation Army in San Antonio, Texas, where she then lived.

The Salvation Army helped by giving Tillie material, thread, zippers, and buttons that were donated to them. Tillie purchased trim, thread, and patterns from her retirement pay. She tried to make each dress different, using fancy braid on one, lace on another. Once in a while, someone would snap a picture of a child wearing the new dress and send it to Tillie. The joy on the child's face encouraged her to work still harder. Once, she made eighty fully lined coats when a tailor who was going out of business donated material to her.

After Tillie moved to Houston to be near her son and daughter-in-law, she continued giving her handiwork to the Salvation Army in San Antonio. When her church (Spring Branch Presbyterian) began to help a low-income "village," Tillie started making dresses for children living there. One year, at the age of seventy, Tillie sent them forty-three items.

"The Sewing Angel" produced more than a thousand articles of clothing for needy children since she started what she called her "little hobby to fill the hours." The secretary of a Houston church who received a gift of the handmade dresses wrote Tillie Fisher this thank-you: "I'm sure no one puts more time or effort—as well as love—into a gift than you do."

Time, effort, and love—that was Tillie Fisher's threefold gift to needy children she would never meet.

—Story suggested by Dell Buller

185

# A FLOWERING COUNTRY

Because of the promise a retired New York City restaurateur made to God, the verdant countryside in and around Ulster County, New York, took on added beauty. The reason rested with a man named Manden Toku Ishii, who lived near Kerhonkson, New York, and his skill at growing Japanese cherry trees.

After Mr. Ishii retired, he began to raise cherry trees like the ones he had admired in northern Japan as a boy. Years later, Mr. Ishii fell and fractured his spine. For seven days he lay paralyzed in a hospital, unable to eat, drink, or even talk to visitors.

"There was only one thing I could do: pray," Mr. Ishii recalled. "And I did that every minute. The pain was so great that I finally asked God to take me home with him."

There was one night a short time later when he thought he had gone to heaven, but, he said, "God told me, 'I still have plenty of work for you.'"

And God made the nature of that work very clear. Mr. Ishii described his revelation as being like "lightning in my heart when God told me to recover and make this land a flowering country." Mr. Ishii vowed that he would raise one hundred thousand trees and make gifts of them, if God would give him ten years in which to accomplish it. The bargain seemed to be sealed by Mr. Ishii's complete recovery. Soon he was busily planting row upon row of trees. When they grew, he gave them away to people from all over the United States, and planted more.

His goal of one hundred thousand was surpassed in a little more than six years. Mr. Ishii then set his sights on giving away one million trees—"If God gives me the time to do it."

No spring will dawn without Ulster County residents looking out upon tree after tree of cherry blossoms and remembering a man who promised God he would "make this a flowering country."

# NEIGHBOR ACROSS THE SEA

Dear neighbor across the sea," began the letter pinned to one of the bright sections of cloth. "This quilt is a token of friendship from the women of America."

The message was going to some needy family in Korea or Czechoslovakia, or some other distant part of the world. And the gift they received stemmed from the efforts of Mrs. Aline Hager of Ashland, Kentucky, who for more than twenty years literally blanketed the world with the message of God's love.

In 1946, Mrs. Hager was teaching a mission Sunday school class at South Ashland United Methodist Church in Ashland when she conceived the idea of making "friendship quilts" from scraps of wool and corduroy.

Mrs. Hager embroidered the center square of each quilt with the message, "God Is Love." Then she handed them out to church women of Boyd County, Kentucky, who finished the quilts, which were distributed through Church World Service. About fifty quilts were sent to the needy.

One of the first went to the Zion Methodist Church in Seoul, Korea, and a teenager, Jong Ho Lee, wrote to thank Mrs. Hager.

He told her that the quilt had been given to a penniless young North Korean refugee couple. Jong Ho Lee and Mrs. Hager corresponded, and soon Mrs. Hager's church was sending its love offerings to provide Bibles, pictures, a slide projector, and an education fund for the South Korean church.

Mrs. Hager's concern ministered to the spirit as well as to the body.

When one of the quilts arrived at a church behind the Iron Curtain, the pastor held an all-day service to display it. He wrote to Mrs. Hager, "Your friendship letter was like balm to an aching world."

—Story suggested by Ruth Power Pond

# SAUCEPAN SAINTS

first heard the phrase "saucepan saints" used by a visiting evangelist who preached in my church when I was young. But it wasn't until the day my husband died that I understood its full meaning.

The woman who stood at my front door that day didn't look angelic or saintly, just kind and motherly. I recognized her as Margaret Nebzydoski, one of the older members of my church, Holiday Hills Baptist. Although she taught adult Sunday school and had been president of the Women's Missionary Union for three years, most often she was busy at the stove before a church supper or a WMU reception.

She put her arms around me and said quietly, "I can't say pretty words to take away the hurt. But I was widowed young myself, and I know how you feel. If you will just lead me to the kitchen, maybe I can help a little. I've always been at home among the pots and pans."

And so she was. She entered the kitchen with an air of confidence. Quickly she sized up the stove and other utilities. Then

190

she went to the telephone and began alerting other saucepan saints.

Within a short time, these good women appeared at my door, laden with cakes, salads, chicken, and vegetables—all fixed in a tempting manner. Many of these women shrank from teaching a Sunday school class, but they were all dynamos in the kitchen. They prepared meals, while scores of people milled in and out to offer condolences. Even the day of the funeral, twenty people were fed without too much difficulty.

In the sad hours that followed, I was comforted many times by Mrs. Nebzydoski's kindly way of appearing just before lunch or supper with some dish or cakes. For one solid week, I did not cook. When my refrigerator flowed over, she quietly removed the leftovers and took them to her own home, labeled them, and placed them in her own freezer to await my need of them.

Weeks later, when I ate these dishes, I breathed a prayer of relief and gratitude for women like Margaret Nebzydoski, who have consecrated their stoves and kitchens, and who serve from saucepans liberally spiced with Christian love and concern.

—Joanne L. Pope